MW00340484

EAT, DRINK,
and BE MURRAY

EAT, DRINK, and BE MURRAY

A FEAST OF FAMILY FUN AND FAVORITES

ANDY MURRAY

DEYST.

An Imprint of WILLIAM MORROW

TO MOM AND DAD,
who gave me life,

AND TO MY SON, DREW,
who gave my life purpose

CONTENTS

FOREWORD

Hello, are you hungry? Ready to eat?

May I suggest a glass of water to stave off impulse eating.

Because when I read a cookbook, I get hungry and often can't wait to prepare something worthy of my years on earth let alone what's in the cookbook I'm reading. This one is even more suggestive than most: The recipes of my childhood, and those my talented chef brother Andy earned in his years in professional kitchens.

These meals aren't just calories for the body, but memories, emotions, and feelings remembered upon entering the nose and mouth. There are photographs too, which lower my shoulders and my hips into my chair, of loved ones gone and loved ones all growed up. In a large family, someone always stood by the cook, my mother, collecting reflected love directed at the pots and pans. The visible reward for this shared companionship was the first finished morsel of the dish. And with the first taste and chews came Mom's alert, "Is that table set?" With that question energy appeared to carry out the task.

"Nancy!"

"I put out the forks."

"Peggy!"

"I put out the glasses and all the plates."

"Brian!"

"I put out the spoons and knives."

"Edward!"

"I'm pouring the milk."

"Billy! Billy!"

"I'm standing right next to you; I'm going to carry the platter."

Child after child assembles by the stove.

"Dinner is ready."

The father enters and leads the blessing, then a child's voice, "God bless the cook." Then another, "And the one who buys the food."

Andy's my little brother. Not the littlest, but littler. So many lovely, lovable brothers and sisters, and if you're littler—some special you, must raise its voice to be heard above that din.

And by the stove, in the shadow of our mother, is where little Andy learned to love.

BY BILL MURRAY

INTRODUCTION
WHERE IT ALL BEGAN

Lucille and Edward Murray

'VE ALWAYS BELIEVED THAT FOOD IS THE GREAT EQUALIZER. Seriously, think about it. I can't tell you how many times I've seen someone in a bad mood eat a great meal, and then, like magic, the problem takes a back seat. People can be screaming at their cousins about politics on Thanksgiving, and a perfectly cooked turkey with stuffing and gravy will shut it down (at least until everyone is finished with their pumpkin pie).

I've seen it happen with my own eyes, time and time again, so I feel confident saying that food makes us *happy.* Well . . . good food does, anyway, but that's another story. Comfort food is a real thing, and it's very big for me.

My parents were Lucille and Edward (but everyone called him Ed). They were twenty-two when they got married in 1943; and they treated each other with such respect, because they were so in love. My dad was a salesman in the lumber business and came home from work every night at 5:30 P.M. My mom would put down her wooden spoon to greet him at the door, and they would share this long kiss, which is really sweet now that I think about it. Dinner was a big deal in our house, all of us sitting together Sunday through Thursday, *no* exceptions.

Ed and Lucille striking a pose

Mom and Dad were both quite funny—my dad with his dry sense of humor and my mom with her great laugh. There was always a contest to try to get my father to laugh at dinner. If you could get Dad to laugh, it was a big deal.

Our dining room table is legendary to this day—a Duncan Phyfe drop-leaf dining room table with five removable leaves, 41½ inches wide by 127 inches long, comfortably seating nine kids, with Mom and Dad at the heads. The rule was that nobody touched their food until Mom was seated. Then Dad would carefully carve the meat, fill every plate, and pass it down the table. He was big on meat and potatoes and manners, so that's what we usually ate, and absolutely no elbows were allowed on the table. I sat to my father's left, and if I put my elbow on the table for even a second, he'd take the fat end of the knife and bang my elbow with it. We were very old school, but hey, I've been told that my table manners are exceptional, and I owe that to my parents.

My dad had type 1 diabetes and was very thin, so Mom was always trying to fatten him up. She'd put cream in his cereal, extra butter on his potatoes—anything to give him more calories. Mom was always looking out for him. He died on December 29, 1967, due to complications from diabetes, at just forty-six years old. We were fortunate to have our mother in our lives for another twenty-one years. She died of complications from lymphoma on November 2, 1988.

I remember right after Dad died, my mom called a family meeting with us kids. We were all sitting around the dining room table like in the movie *Cheaper by the Dozen* (the original). Mom turned to all us kids and said, "We're all going to

My parents with my sister Nancy,
a year before my dad passed

have to stick together, here." She went back to work for the first time since she was a teenager. We kids ranged in age from twenty-three (Edward) to five (Joel). I was eleven. We knew we would all be leaning on one another more than ever.

There was never a dull moment in the Murray house. I love my siblings more than anything, but, oh man, they can still be a lot to keep up with! From oldest to youngest, it's Edward, Brian, Nancy, Peggy, Billy, Laura, Andy, Johnny, and Joel. (We used to compete to see who could say all our names in a row the fastest.)

All the Murray kids with Lucille

My older brother Edward went to Northwestern University as an Evans Scholar—which is a golf scholarship. He introduced me to my first gin martini at a place called Matty's Wayside Inn. He had a bit of the performer gene in him too, and later on was actually a DJ in Sheboygan, Wisconsin, before getting into radio sales. One of his first jobs was with television pioneer Lee Philips, where he got to meet people like the great Phyllis Diller. As you might've guessed from him being an Evans Scholar, his favorite pastime was golf. He could remember every game and describe each hole, shot by shot. He loved to sing (although he didn't always have the best pitch) and would gladly get onstage at our charity golf tournament to sing "New York, New York." We lost Edward in November 2020. I miss him dearly.

Brian is just a year younger than Edward, and he is thoughtful, kind, and sincere. He has made quite a name for himself working as a writer and character actor (I chuckle every time I see him as the crabby boss in

Christmas Vacation). A lot of people don't know he was a member of the Second City before Billy even thought about acting, and it was Brian who encouraged Billy to start taking classes. He also became a writer and featured player on *Saturday Night Live* in the 1980s. Another fun fact: A photographer captured an image of Brian eating Cracker Jack when he was about four years old, and it wound up in *Life* magazine. We always joke that

Lucille, Ed, and Edward

he was my mother's favorite because he was the smallest baby.

Nancy, also known as "Sister Nancy" to her students and "Nancy the Nun" to everyone else, will be the first to tell you that she's the only person in the family with a degree in drama. (She's also the only nun. She does a one-woman show about Catherine of Siena, but that's for another time.) She taught drama to Catholic high school students and then spent twenty years working at St. Sylvester Church in Humboldt Park, at the time one of the most

Nancy and Brian

dangerous neighborhoods in Chicago. Oh, and don't count on her to arrive on time, because she is always late. But when she does make it, she can be very entertaining. Nancy taught herself to play piano by ear, so when she plays songs on Christmas Eve, it's always a treat.

I call my sister Peggy the CEO of all things Murray. Not only is she a total doll, but she's thoughtful too. Peggy knows what we all want for Christmas, and she makes

That's Peggy in the front with Bill, Laura, Nancy, and Santa.

sure everyone is included for family gatherings. She's also a wonderful cook, with the perfect kitchen for entertaining. Because she's the family CEO and a top chef, we often go to her house for the holidays. She's also the connector—making sure people stay in touch. I know I'm in touch with her a *lot* about cooking. Her opinion is number one, as far as I'm concerned!

Bill (the family calls him Billy) is one of the most generous people you will ever meet in your entire life, but you will never know about it from him. He's a humble guy, doesn't like to brag. Unless we're talking about the Chicago Cubs—our whole family is diehard for that team. I guess sports have always been a huge part of our lives. He was my basketball coach when I was in fourth grade and he was sixteen, and

Billy with John Candy onstage with the Second City

Billy at high school graduation

we were always shooting baskets in the driveway. Billy's not big on cooking—he would rather starve than slave away in the kitchen, so I've gladly stepped in over the years to make sure Thanksgiving or Christmas dinners are done right. When Bill is in a great mood, there's nobody else in the world you would rather be with. When Billy's in a bad mood, you don't want to be in the same city.

Me with Laura and Dad

Laura is the sweetest girl I've ever met. She reminds me so much of my mom, both in her looks and personality. She's very considerate of people's feelings, and she makes everyone feel at home. We have always been really close because there isn't another sibling between us in the birth order. She also drove me everywhere because she got her license before I did, so we did a lot of bonding in the car while singing songs from the 1960s. She and her husband, Bob, are the best hosts, with incredible attention to detail and presentation. They have always welcomed me to their home when I visit Chicago, and I just adore them both.

Johnny and Laura

Johnny and I are just two years apart and were inseparable growing up. When I was in a phase of thinking I would be a baseball pitcher, Johnny said he would be my catcher. I would throw pitches to him in the backyard all day long. We got into a lot of trouble sneaking across the street to the garden in the convent and helping ourselves to fruit from their trees

Me with Johnny and Joel on Halloween

Me and Joel

(more on that in chapter 3). Don't tell Billy and Brian I said this—or, if either of you is reading this, just skip over to the next sentence—Johnny may be the funniest guy in the family. He always had us in stitches at the dinner table. He acted for a while but never took it as seriously as Billy, Brian, and Joel.

Joel and I have an interesting relationship because I was his basketball and football coach when he was younger (between fourth and eighth grades). I started coaching when I was fifteen and stopped when I was twenty. Joel was the quarterback, and he was really good. Mr. Stubbs was his nickname— after the chimpanzee in the movie *Toby Tyler*, which is about a kid who runs away to the circus. (When Joel was a baby, he had a pouting lip like the chimp in that movie, so Billy gave Joel the nickname and it just stuck.) He's a seriously trained improv actor, and he can hold his own with the best of them. He's loyal, and he can be very sarcastic too, but Joel is always looking out for everybody.

But really, my love of food—and family—came from my mother. Lucille was the greatest. Everybody felt at home when they sat at her table. Whether it was a celebrity like John Belushi (more on that in chapter 6) or the neighbor next door, Mom made everyone feel special. My friends and cousins would come over to share their woes because she was such a good listener. She was also a good cook and did an amazing job finding creative ways to keep us all fed. Mom always had at least six loaves of bread in the house—either Wonder or Butternut (sometimes Roman Meal would sneak in there too). Sure, there was plenty of summer sausage and bologna to go around, but her go-to trick to hold us over until Dad got home for dinner was peanut butter and mayonnaise sandwiches with iceberg lettuce. No joke. It's actually a delicious combination.

You may be shaking your head, but to this day, if you make any of my brothers a peanut butter, lettuce, and mayo sandwich, they will stop whatever they're doing and eat it right there on the spot. Back then, we used Miracle Whip, but as we got older, we switched to Hellmann's (called Best Foods west of the Mississippi). To some, it may sound horrible, but when you combine the crispiness of the iceberg and the crunch of the peanut butter, it really hits the spot. (We usually used crunchy Skippy, by the way. Occasionally Jif.) I still eat those sandwiches quite often.

When I was about four, my mom was making breakfast, and she looked at me and said, "Andy, it's time for you to learn to make the bacon."

I'd watched her do it so many times I figured I could pull it off.

Mom

"There's one rule," she said, handing me the tongs. "You never leave the room when you're making bacon because as soon as you do, it will burn."

She was right.

It might've been my first time cooking, but I took it very seriously. I learned to cook bacon on medium heat, starting in a cold pan, flipping and watching (and never leaving the room). That was my job, and I was good at it. Eventually, I would graduate to making the eggs in the bacon drippings. Breakfast has always been my favorite meal. Maybe it's because that's where I learned if you're cooking, you get first pick of the bacon . . .

My first restaurant job was at the age of eleven, when I was hired to be the busboy at the corner restaurant called Parker's. I quickly moved up to dishwasher. By the time I was fourteen, I had become a short-order cook. I was making eggs, French toast, hamburgers; you name it, I could crank it out.

After several restaurant jobs close to home, I eventually left the Midwest and made my way to New York for some actual training in my early twenties (graduating with highest honors from the New York Restaurant School). I cooked in some of the busiest kitchens in New York—from La Terrace in the Hamptons to the fabled Mortimer's restaurant in Manhattan. The best experience you can get is from being in the thick of it.

In the kitchen at
Mortimer's, circa 1985

Mortimer's in Manhattan was *the* place to be, back in the day. I saw old money, new money, celebrities from Broadway to the big screen, models, even royalty—basically, if you wanted to be with the in crowd, you came to Mortimer's. I cooked for the king of Spain, Princess Margaret, Frank Sinatra, and Jackie O. (Curious to know how the princess liked her lamb? That's in chapter 6.)

While food has always been a passion of mine, another pastime I enjoy whenever possible is golf. Since my childhood, I've always been around golf courses. I guess that's thanks to Edward. He loved to golf and was really good at it. All my brothers and I spent time caddying at the Indian Hill Club, which was an affluent members-only country club in the northern suburbs of Chicago. I was about ten years old when I started lugging around

All of us on Peggy's stairs at Christmas

clubs to make some money. Brian was so inspired by the characters you find in and around the golf course that he wrote *Caddyshack*, which premiered in 1980, when he was in his early thirties. That movie also inspired some of the items on our restaurant menu at Murray Bros. Caddyshack, which I will be sharing in this book.

My hope in reliving some of my favorite culinary experiences with you over the following pages is that not only will you learn to make some incredible dishes for friends and family but you will also discover your own love of cooking. These stories, recipes, and tips became a part of my DNA after spending a life in the kitchen. Professionally and personally, the kitchen is my "happy place." And while I do think I am the best cook in the Murray family, my sister Peggy can definitely give me a run for my money. You'll see a few of her recipes in here too, so you can decide for yourself. Between milestone celebrations, family holidays, and even cooking after a funeral (just wait till chapter 8), we can put aside all our differences to enjoy a fabulous meal.

Food really is the glue that brings us all together, so let's get ready to *Eat, Drink, and Be Murray*!

1

KITCHEN
ESSENTIALS

That's me, striking a pose
in front of our tree.

CHRISTMAS IN CONNECTICUT

In 1981, my brother Brian decided to do Christmas at his house in New Preston, Connecticut.

"What do you think of cooking that weekend?" he asked.

"Sure!" I responded.

It was a great house. It came with a lot of history. Supposedly George Washington had slept there. Mom, Billy, Johnny, Laura, Joel, Nancy, and a couple of people who lived in the neighborhood showed up for my Christmas meal. Designer Bill Blass lived up the street, and we saw him whenever we would visit. That year, the temperature was about −15°F—the

BRIAN'S MURRAY MEMORY

I loved my house in Connecticut. When the family came for Christmas, what woke me up on Christmas morning was the incredible smell—Andy had taken the peels of the apples and oranges and put them on top of the wood-burning stove (not directly on a burner, but just resting on the warm stove). They gave off this aroma all throughout the house. That was such a clever way to get the house to smell so good. And I was just astonished that he made these quiches for us for breakfast. Then later on we had turkey dinner with all the trimmings. It made me appreciate my two-hundred-year-old farmhouse even more.

coldest Christmas on record at the time. You've never seen so much wood being burned. Between the fireplaces and wood-burning stove, we went through *so much* wood. It was nuts.

In Brian's Connecticut kitchen (you can see the orange and apple peels on the stove behind me)

I'd never cooked on a wood-burning stove before. There was quite a learning curve. You basically have to put wood in the stove every hour to keep it going at a steady 400°F. That meant several of us stayed up all night to keep the fires stoked (and a few of us *may* have put on snowshoes and walked to the liquor store to get more Baileys and Rémy Martin). I made breakfast, lunch, and dinner on that stove; turkey and stuffing, green beans almondine, and pies for dessert. I baked quiche in the morning for brunch. I'd started working at Mortimer's six months prior, so I brought all their equipment with me (unbeknownst to the owner)—blenders, whisk, knives. That's when I realized how important it is to have the right equipment in your kitchen.

That Christmas was when I think my family discovered I could actually cook. They'd only really had my cooking at Parker's Grill, which was a diner. Later, I had worked at a couple of French restaurants in New York, but most of my family wasn't in New York, and the ones who were—Brian and Billy—didn't really hang out in fancy French restaurants. By the time I did Christmas in Connecticut, I'd learned a couple of things, and the Murray family ate very well that holiday. We had a ball. If you're ever saddled with the responsibility of feeding a brood for the first time, I don't recommend trying to pull it off on a wood-burning stove. But if you are going to be entertaining, here are some much-needed items to ensure your success.

JOEL'S FAVORITE CHRISTMAS IN CONNECTICUT MEMORY

Designer Bill Blass had commercials running on television that Christmas season, and every time one would come on, Billy would open the front door and yell down the street, "Bill, you're on channel 2!" About midnight that night, we were all cuddled under blankets, drinks in hand, watching *Saturday Night Live*—it was a rerun that night. Billy entered a scene. Just then, we heard from down the street, in a voice not quite as loud as Billy's, "Bill, you're on channel 4!" Bill Blass may have had the biggest laugh that night.

The table is ready in Connecticut. *From left to right:* That's me, Nancy, Lucille, Johnny, Joel, and Brian. (Nice beard, Johnny!)

MY KITCHEN MUST-HAVES

PANS

It's really important to love your pans. I have two 12-inch skillets that I use daily—a nonstick and a cast iron. The beauty of the nonstick is . . . well, it's self-explanatory. Nonstick pans are also much easier to clean, and if you want to show off, they're good for flipping food—pancakes, omelets, whatever. I also keep a smaller 8-inch nonstick around to whip up eggs in a flash. Now, cast-iron pans are my preference for quality, because

Some of my kitchen essentials

they're virtually indestructible. How many items in the kitchen can you say *that* about? So, the downsides: Cast-iron pans are heavy and cumbersome and a little more difficult to clean. But the way these pans hold heat and flavor the food makes them worth it to me. Honestly, if I had a choice to own only one, it would be a 10-inch cast-iron skillet. As for sauces and gravies (or reheating soup in small quantities), one 2- or 3-quart and one 8- to 10-quart saucepan will serve you well. Pretty much all the recipes in this book can be made with the pans listed above.

DUTCH OVEN

The Dutch oven will make many appearances in this book. It's a must-have because it can be used either in the stove or on the stovetop as a slow cooker. It is heavy and oven safe, and distributes heat evenly. From soups and stews to the main dish, it's versatile and reliable. The price tags run the gamut for this item, but I will say this: Invest in a good Dutch oven, and it will last for generations.

GET TO THE POINT

The two most important knives to own are a chef's knife (usually 8 or 10 inches long) and a paring knife (3 or 4 inches long). Some people think you need the most expensive knife in the store, but that's not true. What you need is a *sharp* knife. Some poorly made knives can't really be sharpened, so they're not efficient. A blunt knife makes it more difficult to cut up your food, *and* if you need to exert more pressure to get results, you're more likely to injure yourself. My advice? Buy a sharpener to keep your knives in top shape.

NOT ALL BOARDS ARE ALIKE

You definitely need a cutting board in your kitchen. These days, I see a lot of people swiping out wood cutting boards for plastic, but I have to tell you this is a really bad idea. What people don't realize is that bacteria can get inside the cuts of a plastic board. This means you must sanitize them very thoroughly *every* time you use them. I prefer wood cutting boards, which seal up more easily, so when you do cut into them they're not as hard to clean. Dish soap will work, but I prefer to mix up a little vinegar, salt, and lemon to clean them up just right.

WHISKY BUSINESS

There are several kinds of whisks—from metal to silicone. I prefer a medium metal whisk—but because a metal whisk will scratch up a nonstick pan, it's best to have a silicone whisk in your repertoire too. Use your whisk to whip eggs, sauces, mashed potatoes, pancake batter, and more. My whisk gets a lot of use.

OUT OF THE GRATE

I encourage cooks to always think outside the box with their grater because it can really come in handy, and not many chefs make full use of their graters.

You may be surprised to know that they aren't just for cheese; you can also use them for lemon peel, garlic, and nutmeg. Graters come in many shapes and sizes. A box grater, which has four sides of different grating ratios and a handle on top, is the most common. There are also Microplane graters, which I use more often. These have a handle and are shaped in a long, thin rectangle. I prefer the Microplane graters because they can be used quickly, adding flavor right into the skillet as you cook. In seconds, you can add lemon zest to a dish to brighten it. But as long as you have some kind of grater, you'll be able to shred like the best of them.

LOVIN' SPOONFUL

The wooden spoon is the tool my mother used to break up fights in the kitchen between the brothers. I'd say I use it more for cooking. In fact, it might be the item that gets the most use in my kitchen. When I put eggs into a nonstick skillet, I move them around with the spoon so as not to scratch the pan like I might with a metal spatula. A wooden spoon is handy in any recipe when it comes to stirring. I keep two types of wooden spoons around—one slotted and one regular.

PINCH ME, I'M DREAMING

I would be lost without my tongs. Now, there are a bunch of different kinds—metal, silicone tipped, and so on. You should own one of each, but if you have to choose only one, I prefer stainless steel. In my mind, the best ones have a spring so you can lock them closed when they're put in the dishwasher. Like Dutch ovens, tongs are a good investment because you can use them for everything—cooking bacon, pulling potatoes out of the oven, even pulling things out from under the broiler. I use tongs when blending pasta into a sauce. It's like having a superhuman hand. Invest in high-quality tongs, and you won't regret it.

CLEAR YOUR SPACE

Chefs hate clutter—at least the good ones do. Always have your work area/station/counter clean when you start your preparation, and be sure to clean as you go (and of course after you finish the meal). My rule is, if I do the cooking, someone else has to wash the dishes. (Maybe it's from all those years of taking turns doing dishes for eleven Murrays while growing up! If I never have to wash another dish, that would be just fine.) Hopefully you have someone in your life who will make that trade with you. This way, everyone can participate, regardless of your experience level in the kitchen.

SPICE UP YOUR PANTRY

SALT AND PEPPER

While lots of folks use sea salt these days, kosher salt is my preference. Because the crystals are larger than those of table salt, you can control the quantity and therefore the flavor more easily. Freshly ground black pepper

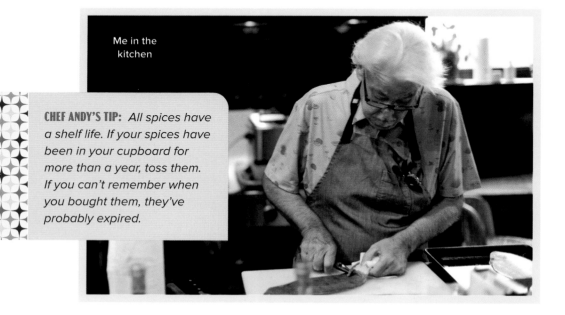

Me in the kitchen

CHEF ANDY'S TIP: *All spices have a shelf life. If your spices have been in your cupboard for more than a year, toss them. If you can't remember when you bought them, they've probably expired.*

is your best bet—I like to use a grinder, and now they even sell pepper in disposable grinders. Freshly ground black pepper is a must in every kitchen.

GARLIC POWDER

When you don't have time to chop your garlic, grab the garlic powder, add a few shakes, and you're set. It's easier to use for garlic bread, and I use it on my roasted pork. It doesn't burn and adds a ton of flavor.

BASIL

Fresh is always best, but if you can't get it fresh, a shaker of dried basil is something you want to have on hand. It's perfect for finishing off pastas and sprinkling on salads.

THYME

I use thyme in most of my French and Italian dishes. You can add it to a spice rub and put it on meats, fish, soups, and anything savory.

OREGANO

I sprinkle oregano on all my Italian food and on most meats and fish too. It's also good for you, as most Italians will tell you, with its anti-inflammatory benefits, just like garlic.

CRUSHED RED PEPPER FLAKES

If you like spice and heat, you can put these flakes on anything you want. They can go in tomato sauce and on pizza and potatoes. I've even been known to shake them on eggs.

CAYENNE

Cayenne peppers are hotter than jalapeños and milder than habaneros. You need only a pinch of dried cayenne, or you can ruin the flavor of your dish, so use it sparingly.

2

OVER
EASY

THE BEST PART OF WAKING UP . . .

When my mother put bacon in the skillet, she literally threw the whole clumped-together pound in there all at once. Sounds like more work, but sure enough, the pieces would start to slide off one by one, and the entire house smelled delicious within minutes.

If we weren't having bacon for breakfast, we were usually eating cereal. We had a charge account at Pearson's, the small grocery store down the street, and on Saturday mornings, Johnny, Laura, and I would go to the grocery store with Mom.

"Pick out what cereal you like," she would say. We each got to choose one box. Sugar Pops was my favorite (later named Corn Pops because of health concerns over promoting sugar, I guess). Cap'n Crunch was a close second.

Joel at our dining room table

We would come back from the store and pour ourselves bowls of cereal and watch cartoons for hours. As you can imagine, in a house with nine kids, those boxes never lasted long.

> Whenever you can—pick up the tab for breakfast. It's the cheapest meal of the day.
>
> —JOEL MURRAY

Some of my favorite memories are about breakfast, especially on Sundays and especially making bacon—okay, *eating* bacon—and spending time together at the table. If you didn't get to the table early enough on Sunday, all the coffee cake and bacon would be gone. And like I said, making bacon really ignited my passion for cooking (and I guess also for eating).

Put it this way: I'm usually the first one in the kitchen.

Of course, my menu has expanded since I was a kid, now including the killer Murray French Toast (page 26) and the savory favorite Chicken Hash (page 28).

When my son was very young, he would call the first meal of the day "breffest." I still joke that a "great breffest" is the only way to start your day. I found some creative ways to get him to eat a healthy breffest, and this chapter includes a couple of his favorites. And after all this time, I can still say breakfast is my favorite meal because it tees you up for the rest of the day, and it never hurts to have your house smell like bacon.

Here are some of my favorite breakfast meals.

MURRAY FRENCH TOAST

SERVES 6 TO 8 • **PREP TIME:** 5 minutes • **COOK TIME:** 10 minutes
TOTAL TIME: 15 to 20 minutes (a couple extra minutes for thicker bread)

French toast was a special-occasion kind of treat for us when we were kids. We never had it during the week, just for the holidays or on the occasional weekend. We used to make this with a loaf of Wonder Bread or Butternut, and I'll still use that from time to time. For the most part, though, I've upgraded my bread to challah or brioche, and I recommend that you do too—it really boosts the flavor and adds texture. If you're hosting brunch, you can make this dish ahead of time and then just keep the toast warm in the oven. The two key ingredients for good French toast are vanilla extract and cinnamon. This dish is easy to make, but I will say that even as an adult, it can make any morning feel special. All the best parts of being a kid again!

6 large eggs

2 cups whole or 2% milk

¼ cup orange juice

½ teaspoon vanilla extract

1 teaspoon sugar

½ teaspoon ground cinnamon

Dash of ground nutmeg

4 tablespoons (½ stick) unsalted butter

8 slices challah, thick white, or brioche bread

Softened butter, for serving

1 cup warm pure maple syrup, for serving

1. In a medium bowl, whisk the eggs. Add the milk, orange juice, vanilla, sugar, cinnamon, and nutmeg and whisk to combine. Set aside.

2. In a large skillet over medium heat, melt 1 tablespoon of the butter.

3. Dip 1 slice of the bread into the egg mixture and place in the skillet. Repeat with a second slice. Fry each side for 2 to 3 minutes, until golden brown. Remove to a plate and lightly cover with foil to keep warm while you continue panfrying the remaining slices of bread. You can also keep the slices warm in a 200°F oven.

4. Serve with softened butter and warm syrup.

CHICKEN HASH

SERVES 4 TO 6 • **PREP TIME:** 15 to 20 minutes • **COOK TIME:** 10 to 15 minutes • **TOTAL TIME:** 25 to 35 minutes

This is a fancy variation on the chipped beef on toast that the army served. Glen, the owner of Mortimer's, first had chicken hash at the famed 21 Club in Manhattan and decided we *must* have it for our brunch menu. Now, what we *didn't* say on the menu is that this dish is a wonderful cure for a hangover (that's why I've suggested it as the main dish in my Hangover Cure menu on page 186). The reason it helps your hangover is, you've got your bread, you've got your meat, you've got your sauce . . . and it just works. I'm sure it's not scientifically proven, but trust me on this one. I've put together a variation on what we served at Mortimer's—it's a little fancier but just as delicious.

2 tablespoons unsalted butter

2 tablespoons all-purpose flour

2 cups whole milk

2 dashes of Tabasco sauce

1 tablespoon Worcestershire sauce

Kosher salt

¼ teaspoon freshly ground black pepper

½ cup heavy cream

¼ cup dry sherry

2 ounces Swiss or Gruyère cheese, grated (about ½ cup)

2 large egg yolks, beaten

2 cups medium diced poached chicken breast

2 ounces Parmesan cheese, grated (about ½ cup)

8 to 12 slices of your favorite toasted bread

1. Preheat the oven broiler to high.

2. In a medium saucepan over medium heat, melt the butter. Slowly whisk in the flour until smooth. Whisk constantly—it will burn fast if you don't keep an eye on it.

3. Slowly pour in the milk and continue whisking until the mixture is thick and smooth. Stir in the Tabasco sauce, Worcestershire sauce, salt, pepper, heavy cream, sherry, and Swiss cheese. Mix until well combined and the cheese is melted.

4. Whisk in the beaten egg yolks until combined. Add the chicken and stir to coat.

5. Transfer the chicken mixture to a baking dish and top with the Parmesan. Place under the broiler and broil until golden brown, about 5 minutes.

6. Serve a healthy spoonful of the chicken hash on top of each slice of toast.

CHEF ANDY'S NOTE: *You can spice this up with different hot sauces if you want to kick up the heat.*

EGGS IN A BASKET

SERVES 2 • **PREP TIME:** 5 minutes • **COOK TIME:** 10 minutes • **TOTAL TIME:** 15 minutes

This is my son Drew's favorite "breffest." It's a good way to get any kid to eat protein, because it *looks* fun. You can use any shape of cookie cutter, making the toast into hearts, stars, or even a Christmas tree (that one is a big hit around the holidays). And don't worry—grown-ups like this dish too. Joel is a big fan and calls it "egg in the hole" or "one-eyed Suzie."

Me and Drew

2 slices bread, anything goes

2 tablespoons unsalted butter, at room temperature

2 large eggs

Kosher salt and freshly ground black pepper

1. Using a sharp, round cookie cutter or the rim of a glass, cut out the centers of both slices of bread. Butter both sides of the bread, including the cutouts.

2. In a medium or large skillet over medium-high heat, melt the remaining butter.

3. Place both pieces of bread—including cut-out pieces—on the skillet. Cook until golden brown, 1 to 2 minutes.

4. Flip the bread and cutouts. One at a time, carefully break the eggs into the holes of the bread slices. Sprinkle with salt and pepper. Reduce the heat to medium and cook for 2 to 3 minutes. Serve with the cutouts on the side.

EGGS BENEDICT

SERVES 2 • **PREP TIME:** 20 minutes • **COOK TIME:** 5 minutes • **TOTAL TIME:** 25 minutes

This dish is a breakfast staple, but the key is the homemade hollandaise sauce. Lots of people switch out their pork bacon for turkey bacon, which is totally fine, but I prefer Canadian bacon. When in season, a beefsteak tomato is a wonderful option in place of the Canadian bacon.

PS: If you're a newer cook, don't be intimidated about poaching an egg. That's the easiest part.

PPS: Might I recommend a slice of beefsteak tomato *and* bacon? Best of both worlds . . .

Consuming raw eggs can be risky. If you are concerned, you can use an egg substitute.

FOR THE HOLLANDAISE SAUCE

8 tablespoons (1 stick) unsalted butter

4 large egg yolks

1½ tablespoons fresh lemon juice

½ teaspoon kosher salt, plus more to taste

Pinch of cayenne pepper or dash of Tabasco sauce

FOR THE EGGS BENEDICT

2 English muffins

2 tablespoons unsalted butter

4 slices Canadian bacon

2 teaspoons white wine vinegar

4 large eggs

1 teaspoon chopped fresh parsley

1. Make the hollandaise sauce: In a medium saucepan over low heat, melt the butter, making sure you do not brown it.

2. Place the egg yolks, lemon juice, and salt in a blender and blend on medium-high for 20 to 30 seconds. The eggs will become lighter yellow in color and will cook enough due to the heat of the butter that's added next.

continued

3. Reduce the blender speed to the lowest setting and slowly dribble in the melted butter while blending. Add the cayenne and blend in. Season to taste with more salt.

4. Set aside in a small container or leave in the blender until ready for use.

5. Make the eggs Benedict: Split and toast the English muffins. Butter each half with ½ tablespoon of the butter. Place on a serving plate.

6. In a small skillet over medium heat, lightly brown the Canadian bacon on both sides, about 90 seconds on each side. Remove and place a slice on each English muffin half. Set aside.

7. Fill a medium saucepan halfway with water. Add the vinegar and bring to a boil. Lower to a simmer.

8. Crack 1 egg into a coffee cup or small bowl, then slowly slide it into the simmering water. Once the egg starts forming its shape, repeat the process with the next egg, until all 4 are in the pan and beginning to take shape. Turn off the heat and cover the pan. Let sit for 4 minutes.

9. With a slotted spoon, remove the eggs one at a time. Try to remove the eggs in the same order you put them in the pan. Using a clean dish towel or paper towel, lightly pat each egg to remove excess water.

10. Place 1 egg on top of each slice of Canadian bacon.

11. Top the eggs with hollandaise sauce, garnish with the parsley, and serve immediately.

BLUEBERRY PANCAKES

SERVES 4 • **PREP TIME:** 15 minutes • **COOK TIME:** 5 minutes • **TOTAL TIME:** 30 minutes (includes resting time)

The first time I experienced fruit in pancakes was when I was in my twenties and living in New York City. My roommate, Mac, and I were both under the weather, and his girlfriend came over and made us pancakes with strawberries. Well, those blew my mind. I was always good at making buttermilk pancakes, but now I can't pass up the chance to put my favorite fruit in there too. The thing with blueberries is that if you add them in the batter, the batter—and the pancakes—will turn purple. So the best way to do it is to ladle the pancake patter into the skillet and then drop 8 to 10 blueberries on each pancake before you flip.

CHEF ANDY'S NOTE: *When you flip the pancakes and the fruit side is down, don't press down or you'll burst the berries!*

2 cups all-purpose flour

2 tablespoons sugar

½ teaspoon baking powder

½ teaspoon baking soda

½ teaspoon kosher salt

2 large eggs

1 cup buttermilk

½ cup whole or 2% milk

2 tablespoons unsalted butter, melted

1 tablespoon unsalted butter or vegetable oil, for greasing

1 pint fresh blueberries

1 cup warm pure maple syrup

1. In a large bowl, whisk together the flour, sugar, baking powder, baking soda, and salt.

2. In a medium bowl, whisk together the eggs, buttermilk, and milk until well combined.

3. Pour the wet ingredients into the bowl with the dry ingredients. Using a whisk or wooden spoon, mix until the batter just comes together. Don't worry if it's slightly lumpy—that actually makes a fluffier pancake.

continued

4. Stir in the melted butter.

5. Let the batter sit for 10 minutes, uncovered.

6. Heat a griddle or large skillet over medium to medium-high heat. Lightly grease the pan with the butter or oil.

7. Ladle ¼ cup of the pancake batter on the griddle. Repeat 2 or 3 more times, depending on the size of the griddle.

8. Place 8 to 10 blueberries on top of each pancake. When air bubbles form, 2 to 3 minutes, flip the pancakes. When the pancake bottoms are golden brown, about 1 minute, remove to a plate and lightly cover with foil to keep warm while you continue cooking. Repeat until the remaining batter is gone, adding butter to the pan as needed.

9. Serve hot with warm maple syrup on the side.

3

SMALL PLATES AND SIDES

HOME IS WHERE THE HEART IS

Mom and Dad with (*from left*) Billy, Brian, Edward, me, Nancy, Peggy, and Laura

The Murrays grew up in the Chicago area, in a suburb called Wilmette, which is about thirty minutes north of the city along Lake Michigan. Our house was very small, and with so many of us kids, there was a boys' room, a girls' room, and, as the family grew, a baby in a crib with my parents.

We lived right across the street from the Mallinckrodt Convent, Sisters of Christian Charity. Some wonder if that's why my sister Nancy became a nun, but her siblings always felt she was inspired by *The Sound of Music*.

My first exposure to fresh fruit and produce was on the beautiful convent grounds, which consisted of approximately twenty acres. The nuns grew apples, pears, cherries, and strawberries—and there were huge gardens packed with a variety of vegetables.

The head gardener was Sister Friedberta, a woman who spoke German and was very intimidating. Even though we were a little scared of her, there was no denying she did a fabulous job of taking care of the garden. She was assisted by a team of postulants (nuns in training) who worked in the garden every day. It was gorgeous.

My brother Johnny and I used to climb the wall and go rummaging through the garden, helping ourselves to whatever snacks we could find until the nuns would chase us out. We were

The nuns at Mallinckrodt Convent, tending to their garden

Sister Friedberta

always able to outrun the nuns, but we'd drop a lot of apples or strawberries during our escape.

One day, Johnny and I were picking apples and the nuns started chasing us; only this time, I was so weighed down with my stash I couldn't get away fast enough. Sister Friedberta grabbed my shoulder and turned me around. I was terrified. She saw the apple in my hand and said in her German accent, "If you like that, then try this!" She handed me a tomato. And I thought, *No, thanks*. I was sure this was some kind of punishment.

"Eat it like an apple," she commanded.

I'd never eaten anything like it. Ripe and homegrown, it was the best tomato I've ever had in my whole life. I've been searching for "the Great Tomato" ever since. And I'll always be grateful to Sister Friedberta for catching me in the orchard that day!

I love small plates and sides, because—like that one epic tomato—sometimes small bites *are* the best. I'm including some of my family's favorite starters and sides, which you can make for any meal or party. Most of them are used by me (and the siblings) to this day. A get-together is simply not complete without Hot Nuts (page 58), and Peggy's Baked Beans (page 49) will become a staple for you at every barbecue. I am so sentimental about Lucille's Salad (page 53) that she had to have a shout-out in here as well.

But we begin with a tomato pie—remembering the time a stern nun forced me into eating something that was actually *good* for me and that wound up being so delicious.

Twelve years old, at my confirmation

TEMPTING TOMATO PIE

SERVES 6 • **PREP TIME:** 30 minutes • **COOK TIME:** 40 minutes
TOTAL TIME: 1 hour 20 minutes (includes cooling time)

CHEF ANDY'S NOTE: *A pro tip for slicing and dicing: Chiffonade is the simple process of slicing an herb (or other leafy green) into thin ribbons. Stack a few leaves, roll them into a cigar shape, and then slice them into thin strips on a cutting board. You now have attractive ribbons to use as a garnish!*

This could be a snack, an appetizer, or even a full meal if you have no "off switch." And trust me, that option is tempting! Between the mozzarella and the tomatoes, this is like an even more delicious pizza.

One of the key ingredients for this pie is the cheese. Because fresh mozzarella is 52 percent water, if it's not drained, your dish will be watery. So, after slicing the mozzarella, lay it out on paper towels to drain for 15 minutes before putting your pie together. Be sure your tomatoes are ripe for the best flavor.

One 9-inch prebaked pie shell

2 tablespoons Dijon mustard

1 pound fresh mozzarella cheese, thinly sliced

3 pounds ripe tomatoes, thinly sliced

1 tablespoon finely chopped garlic

2 tablespoons finely chopped fresh oregano

Kosher salt and freshly ground black pepper

1 tablespoon extra virgin olive oil

1 tablespoon fresh basil

1. Preheat the oven to 350°F.

2. Brush the bottom and sides of the pie shell with the mustard.

3. Layer the bottom of the pie shell with one third of the mozzarella slices. Arrange one third of the tomatoes on top, then one third of the garlic on top of the tomatoes.

continued

4. Sprinkle 1 tablespoon of the oregano on the tomatoes and garlic, then lightly season with salt and pepper. Top the tomatoes with half of the remaining mozzarella, then half of the remaining garlic.

5. Arrange half of the remaining tomatoes on top of the cheese with the remaining garlic. Season with the remaining 1 tablespoon oregano and another easy sprinkling of salt and pepper.

6. Place the remaining mozzarella on top of the tomatoes, then arrange the final layer of tomatoes on top. Lightly season once more with salt and pepper.

7. Drizzle the top of the pie with the oil.

8. Bake for 40 minutes, or until the cheese on top is melted.

9. Let the pie rest on a cooling rack at room temperature for 10 minutes.

10. Garnish with the basil chiffonade and serve.

CADDYSHACK GOLF BALLS

MAKES 16 GOLF BALLS • **PREP TIME:** 1 hour • **COOK TIME:** 10 to 15 minutes
TOTAL TIME: 2 hours 15 minutes (includes refrigeration time)

While most people consider leftovers to be an afterthought, we found a way to bring them front and center at our restaurant in St. Augustine. It was Vero, one of my best morning cooks, who decided to be creative with some leftover ingredients. She said, "I just made this. What do you think?"

> *I remember reading an interview with John Goodman, and he said never invest in restaurants. There's a 90 percent failure rate. I guess I didn't listen.*
>
> **—BILL MURRAY**

What did I think? It was mashed potatoes, cheese, bacon, onion, and garlic—and it was deep fried. How can you go wrong? Vero sure didn't. We sell thousands of our golf balls a week—people just love 'em, and now you can make them too!

2 pounds russet potatoes

Kosher salt

4 ounces bacon, roughly chopped

½ cup whole milk, warmed

4 ounces Cheddar-Jack cheese, shredded (about 1 cup)

HORSERADISH CREAM SAUCE

½ cup full-fat sour cream

½ cup prepared horseradish

½ cup mayonnaise

1 tablespoon Worcestershire sauce

2 teaspoons chopped fresh dill

Vegetable oil, for frying

4 large egg whites, lightly beaten

1 cup unseasoned bread crumbs

1. Peel and quarter the potatoes. Place them in a large pot with enough cold, well-salted water to cover by an inch. Bring the water to a boil and cook the potatoes until tender, about 20 minutes.

continued

2. In a medium pan over medium heat, cook the bacon until browned, 8 to 10 minutes. Transfer the bacon to a plate lined with paper towels to drain.

3. Drain the potatoes in a colander, then transfer to a large bowl. Mash the potatoes, adding the milk as you mash, until smooth. Stir in the bacon and cheese until well incorporated.

CHEF ANDY'S NOTE: *These golf balls are a great substitute for French fries. You can also make them in a deep fryer or air fryer.*

4. Cover the mashed potatoes and refrigerate for at least 1 hour or up to 3 hours.

5. Make the horseradish cream sauce: In a medium bowl, mix together the sour cream, horseradish, mayo, Worcestershire sauce, and dill. Refrigerate until the golf balls are ready to serve.

6. In a large Dutch oven, heat at least 3 inches of vegetable oil to 350°F.

7. While the oil is heating, set up a dredging station with the egg whites in one wide, shallow bowl or pie plate and the bread crumbs in another.

8. Remove the mashed potatoes from the refrigerator. Using a small ice cream scoop or clean hands, shape the mixture into balls the size of golf balls. Roll 1 ball in the egg whites, shaking off any excess, then in the bread crumbs to evenly coat. Place on a baking sheet, then continue with the remaining balls.

9. Working in batches, carefully place the golf balls in the hot oil with a slotted spoon one at a time. Do not overcrowd. Turn the balls as they brown, 2 to 3 minutes per side. When the balls are golden brown on all sides, they are done, 5 to 7 minutes.

10. Serve hot with the horseradish cream sauce on the side.

CHEF ANDY'S NOTE:
Seriously, don't mess with this recipe. Peggy will find you.

PEGGY'S BAKED BEANS

SERVES 6 • **PREP TIME:** 15 minutes • **COOK TIME:** 8 hours • **TOTAL TIME:** 8 hours 15 minutes

The first time I had my sister Peggy's baked beans, I was in high school. She couldn't make enough of them. Everybody went crazy for these beans—they could be our entire meal. So finally I asked her for the recipe, and when she told me, I thought, *This is way too easy.* I couldn't believe it. When I got older, I was hosting a party in New York and Peggy said, "Don't go changing things in that recipe." I was a chef, so I wanted to add some tomatoes because I just thought it might be dry without them. I felt it just needed *something* because there were so few ingredients. *How could it be so simple?* Well, I didn't listen. And it didn't turn out well. When she came over, she took one look at my baked beans and said, "You messed with it, didn't you?" She just knew.

> *Don't f— with the recipe.*
> —**PEGGY**

Be sure to bake this for the entire 8 hours. (Cutting it short in any way will make it watery.) I've even put it in the oven before going to bed, and when I wake up, the whole house smells heavenly.

Five 14-ounce cans vegetarian baked beans (do not drain)

1 pound bacon, cut into 1-inch squares

2 cups packed dark brown sugar

One 16-ounce can whole tomatoes, drained

1. Preheat the oven to 250°F.

2. In an 11 × 13-inch roasting pan, spread 2½ cans of the baked beans evenly on the bottom of the pan.

3. Arrange half of the bacon on top of the beans. Sprinkle 1 cup of the brown sugar on top of the bacon.

4. Repeat the process, layering with the remaining beans, bacon, and brown sugar.

5. Arrange the tomatoes evenly on top.

6. Bake, uncovered, for 8 hours, or until most of the liquid has evaporated. *Do not stir or shorten the cooking time!*

JOHNNY'S MURRAY MEMORY

The meal was not done until the dishes were, and that involved at least four people saying they did them last night or did the lunch dishes, or they had homework or some other important excuse. There were plates, bowls, serving dishes and platters, pots and pans, glasses, and silverware, for eleven people (or more, depending on the guest list). Figure at least an hour-plus of hard work.

We had a dishwashing machine, and I remember it was brown. Also, that I never saw it work. Some of the older kids told stories about the "golden days past" when the dishwasher worked, but apparently it stopped working as soon as I was born (I was eighth out of nine). Only then could you go about your business, be it homework, watching TV, or fighting with your brothers and sisters, then dreaming about the next meal.

The Murray family home in Wilmette, Illinois

RED RADISH SPREAD

SERVES 4 TO 6 • **PREP TIME:** 15 minutes • **ASSEMBLY TIME:** 5 minutes • **TOTAL TIME:** 1 hour 20 minutes

One thing we always had around the holidays were those relish trays, which had olives, radishes, pickles, pretzels, celery, carrots, and maybe some crackers. The majority of the Murray kids would always pick out the olives. I remember when I'd go to my cousin's house, we were always the first ones to clean out the black olives. I could make a meal of them, putting one on each finger. For some reason, Brian went for all the radishes. We'd

Dancing to stay warm during Christmas in Connecticut

let him, because, well . . . more olives for the rest of us. Since he enjoyed them so much, my sister Peggy made a dip with radishes as the main ingredient. It's so simple, and you can put it on crackers, or scoop it up with pretzels. Does it give my beloved olives a run for their money? Okay, yes . . .

One 8-ounce bag trimmed radishes

1 or 2 scallions, white and green parts separated, minced (about 3 tablespoons)

8 ounces cream cheese, softened

8 tablespoons (1 stick) salted butter, softened

½ teaspoon freshly ground black pepper

1. Use a food processor to finely chop the radishes. Transfer to a medium bowl. Add the minced scallion whites and mix well.

2. Place the cream cheese and butter in the food processer (no need to clean it out first), and cream together until mixed.

continued

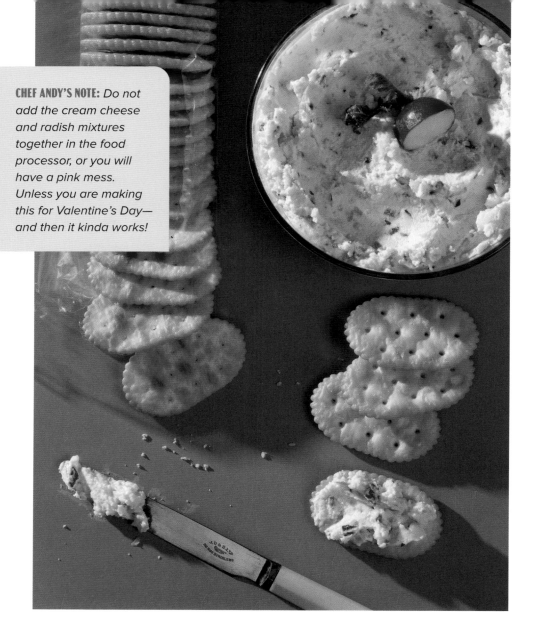

CHEF ANDY'S NOTE: *Do not add the cream cheese and radish mixtures together in the food processor, or you will have a pink mess. Unless you are making this for Valentine's Day— and then it kinda works!*

3. Scrape the cream cheese mixture into the vegetable bowl, add the pepper, and mix well to combine.

4. Cover the bowl and place in the refrigerator for at least 1 hour.

5. When ready to serve, garnish with the reserved scallion greens. Serve with your favorite crackers or toasted bread.

LUCILLE'S SALAD

SERVES 4 TO 6 • **PREP TIME:** 15 minutes • **ASSEMBLY TIME:** 5 to 10 minutes • **TOTAL TIME:** 25 minutes

When we were growing up, our salads were simple—just iceberg lettuce, cucumbers, and scallions. But for special occasions, this salad was Mom's specialty. (At the time, most of our vegetables actually came frozen or from a can, so this was a treat.) You need a soft lettuce for this dish; a combination of butter lettuce, like Bibb, and red leaf lettuce seems to work best with the oranges. And the red leaves pop on the plate. It's sweet, healthy, and always a crowd-pleaser.

It's funny, because by the time I got to Mortimer's, all we served was really good lettuce—that's all the society women from the Upper East Side wanted to eat! These days I love butter lettuce, watercress, and romaine, but give me the choice of a salad, and I'll always choose this one.

continued

NANCY'S MURRAY MEMORY

Mom would often be sitting at the kitchen table peeling potatoes. I think they were a part of most of our meals. There was always a chair to sit on when you came in with the news from school. She would hear about what was served in the cafeteria, who got in trouble, and the good results from a quiz you had studied for the night before; see a new cheer I had learned; or hear a song we had learned in choral. Mom was a great listener.

½ cup canola oil

3 tablespoons red wine vinegar

1 tablespoon fresh lemon juice

2 tablespoons sugar

½ teaspoon dry mustard

½ teaspoon kosher salt

Head of red leaf lettuce

Head of Bibb lettuce

½ medium red onion, thinly sliced

½ teaspoon grated yellow onion

One 11-ounce can mandarin oranges, drained

¼ cup slivered almonds, toasted

1. In a small bowl, whisk together the oil, vinegar, lemon juice, sugar, dry mustard, and salt until emulsified.

2. Wash and dry the lettuces. Tear the leaves into bite-size pieces and place in a large salad bowl.

3. Add both onions, the oranges, and almonds and toss to combine.

4. Drizzle the dressing over the salad and toss again to incorporate.

CORN FRITTERS WITH SALMON ROE

SERVES 2 • **PREP TIME:** 10 minutes • **COOK TIME:** 5 minutes • **TOTAL TIME:** 15 minutes

The first time I had caviar, it was like that scene out of the movie *Big* with Tom Hanks, where he's at the Christmas party, spitting caviar into his napkin. The *aha* moment wouldn't come for me until *way* later, and if it hasn't come for you, these fritters might be the game changer . . .

One day at Mortimer's, our chef, Stephen, said, "Let's do a fritter." Since caviar in any dish wasn't financially responsible, we substituted salmon roe for the caviar. I also removed ingredients such as eggs and milk to make the batter lighter. This is my variation on the fritters we served at Mortimer's.

½ cup all-purpose flour

¼ teaspoon baking powder

Pinch of kosher salt

⅔ cup soda water

1 cup fresh or canned corn

2 teaspoons chopped fresh chives

1 tablespoon vegetable oil

3 ounces salmon roe

2 to 3 tablespoons crème fraîche

1. In a medium bowl, whisk together the flour, baking powder, salt, and half of the soda water until smooth. Add the rest of the soda water, stirring, to create a thin batter.

2. Add the corn and 1 teaspoon of the chives to the batter and mix together.

3. In a large skillet over medium heat, heat the vegetable oil.

4. Place tablespoonsful of the corn mixture—about the size of a silver dollar pancake—into the pan. You should have 6 fritters. Panfry until golden brown and bubbles begin to form, about 4 minutes.

5. Flip and cook the other side until golden brown, about 2 minutes.

6. Transfer the fritters to a plate. Evenly divide the roe among the fritters. Top each fritter with a small dollop of crème fraîche and garnish with the remaining 1 teaspoon chives before serving.

CHEF ANDY'S NOTE: *A good sushi place will have salmon roe, and you can also find it online. As for the corn, fresh corn in season is wonderful, but I've been known to use Green Giant Niblets in a pinch—and I bet you'd be hard pressed to know the difference!*

HOT NUTS

SERVES 6 • **PREP TIME:** 5 minutes • **COOK TIME:** 25 minutes • **TOTAL TIME:** 30 minutes

Another concoction created for social gatherings (especially holidays) was something the Murrays call "hot nuts." Laura makes them on a regular basis. Different versions of this dish have been created over the years at varying households (Joel likes it with jalapeño peppers); and spices, onions, and other items have been added and taken away. But one thing's for sure: It's a great dish for any party, and it's better than having to crack walnuts. My family served it with Triscuit crackers. This is the original version.

Clockwise from left: Johnny, Ed, Andy, Brian, Billy, and Joel with Lucille

8 ounces cream cheese, softened

½ cup full-fat sour cream

½ cup chopped green bell pepper

One 3-ounce package chipped beef, finely diced

2 tablespoons whole milk

2 teaspoons onion flakes

½ teaspoon kosher salt

¼ cup pecans, chopped and toasted

1. Preheat the oven to 350°F.
2. In a large bowl, mix together the cream cheese, sour cream, bell pepper, chipped beef, milk, onion flakes, and salt until well incorporated.
3. Transfer the mixture to a 1-quart oven-safe serving dish.
4. Spoon the pecans over the cheese mixture.
5. Bake until bubbly, about 25 minutes.
6. Serve with your favorite cracker.

CHEF ANDY'S NOTE:
Sometimes my sisters will toast the pecans in 2 tablespoons butter. Let's face it—everything's better with butter.

POTATOES DAUPHINOISE

SERVES 8 TO 10 • **PREP TIME:** 30 to 40 minutes • **COOK TIME:** 1 hour 30 minutes • **TOTAL TIME:** 2 hours 10 minutes

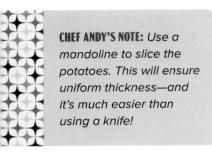

CHEF ANDY'S NOTE: *Use a mandoline to slice the potatoes. This will ensure uniform thickness—and it's much easier than using a knife!*

When I worked at Mortimer's, the owner, Glenn, would say, "Please, don't let anyone touch the potatoes until Andy gets here. He's Irish. He knows potatoes!" We always had potatoes in my house. Mashed potatoes and gravy were the staple side for most dinners. I could eat potatoes and gravy all day long.

When we had company over, Mom would kick the potatoes up a notch and make them au gratin. That was also a common recipe for Easter—ham with au gratin potatoes. We always celebrated Easter at home. My parents really got into hiding baskets of candy for all the kids. (Now that I'm older, I see that it's a really bad idea having nine kids hopped up on sugar Easter morning.)

Potatoes have always been a comfort to me. By the time I was working at La Terrace in Shelter Island, I started to get more creative with the dauphinoise. I tweaked the recipe when I got to Mortimer's, and I've since adjusted the amount of cheese and cream to perfection. And now, my nephews call this dish "Andy's Potatoes."

½ garlic clove

1 tablespoon unsalted butter

3 pounds russet potatoes, peeled and thinly sliced

8 ounces Gruyère or Swiss cheese, shredded (about 2 cups)

Kosher salt and freshly ground black pepper

3 cups heavy cream

1½ ounces Parmesan cheese, grated (about ⅓ cup)

1. Preheat the oven to 400°F.
2. Rub a 2½-quart baking dish with the garlic, then grease with the butter.

3. Shingle one third of the potatoes on the bottom of the dish. Top with one third of the Gruyère. Season with salt and pepper. Repeat for the next two layers.

4. Slowly pour the heavy cream over the top. Top with the Parmesan and cover with foil.

5. Bake for 1 hour. Remove the foil and return to the oven for another 30 minutes, or until the top is golden brown and the potatoes are tender. Allow it to rest for 10 minutes before serving.

4

SENSATIONAL
SOUPS

A MEAL IN A BOWL

When I wasn't in the kitchen cooking, my alter ego was the lead singer for a rock-'n'-roll band. We would do gigs in clubs in New York, and it was a blast. We also performed at Mortimer's famous Fête de Famille party, which helped raise millions for AIDS research. This was the same era when I perfected my recipe for chicken soup.

When I was growing up, soup came out of a can. We had Campbell's tomato soup and sometimes cream of mushroom, never anything fancy. I vividly remember the first time I tried homemade cream of asparagus soup and thinking, *I could get used to this!*

Still, I wasn't a soup guy. Liked it fine, but, well, it was just soup. Where's the excitement? Boy, was I wrong.

Singing with the Andy Murray Band

When I started working in kitchens, I began to appreciate how a good soup could be a game changer. Sure, you can add half a sandwich to really fill you up, but you don't *need* to. I would rather give you more in the bowl so you don't need the sandwich (although some crusty bread on the side for dipping works with each of these recipes—and I recommend *that*).

I've become a soup guy over the years because soup is the ultimate comfort food. Usually easy to make and a satisfying cooking experience too. There's nothing like taking the lid off your pot and getting a whiff of soup. That's when you know that the flavors have all blended together—plus, it makes your house smell amazing. Most people say soups are even better on the second day, but I usually can't wait that long. I'll start it in the morning so the whole house smells delicious, and then I'll reheat it later in the day. You can also freeze these soups (minus the Billi Bi) and pull them out on a cold winter day.

In this chapter, you'll get not only Peggy's Chili (page 69), which is a huge hit even in the summertime, believe it or not, but also some Mortimer's staples that I've tweaked and made my own over the years, like Mortimer's Pistou Soup (page 76) and Billi Bi Soup (page 78)—two items that you'll rarely see on menus. But we'll start off with my legendary chicken soup . . .

ANDY'S CHICKEN VEGETABLE SOUP

SERVES 6 TO 8 • **PREP TIME:** 45 minutes • **COOK TIME:** 1 hour 20 minutes • **TOTAL TIME:** 2 hours 5 minutes

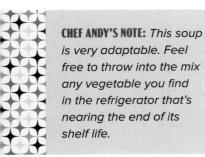

CHEF ANDY'S NOTE: *This soup is very adaptable. Feel free to throw into the mix any vegetable you find in the refrigerator that's nearing the end of its shelf life.*

In the mid-1980s, I was featured in a publication called *Avenue* magazine, which was delivered only to the brownstones on Fifth Avenue and Park Avenue—a very selective crowd. The magazine voted me "One of the 10 Sexiest Men" in Manhattan. Describing one of my signature dating moves, one of the writers said, "When you're sick, Andy brings you chicken soup."

Well, the secret was out—about the soup, I mean. I don't do the traditional "chicken noodle" type of soup. The noodles often get so fat and soggy. I prefer a chicken vegetable soup. Yes, this soup has a lot of ingredients, but don't worry—it's actually quite easy to make.

2 tablespoons unsalted butter

4 ounces button mushrooms, cleaned and sliced

2 tablespoons vegetable oil

1 medium zucchini, cut into ½-inch dice

1 large yellow onion, cut into ½-inch dice

2 celery stalks, cut into ½-inch dice

2 carrots, cut into ½-inch dice

2 garlic cloves, minced

One 15-ounce can whole tomatoes, chopped, with their juice

1 quart chicken stock

1 tablespoon concentrated chicken-base bouillon or 1 chicken bouillon cube

1 tablespoon fresh thyme, chopped

2 skinless, boneless chicken breast halves (6 to 8 ounces each)

1 russet potato, peeled and cut into ½-inch dice

2 cups roughly chopped arugula

½ cup frozen peas

2 tablespoons red wine vinegar

Kosher salt and freshly ground black pepper

continued

1. In a large Dutch oven over medium heat, melt the butter. Add the mushrooms and sauté until lightly browned, about 5 minutes.

2. Transfer the mushrooms to a medium bowl and set aside.

3. Add the oil and sauté the zucchini until lightly browned, about 5 minutes. Transfer to the bowl with the mushrooms.

4. Add the onion, celery, and carrots and sweat for 10 minutes.

5. Add the garlic and sauté until fragrant, about 1 minute.

6. Add the tomatoes, chicken stock, chicken bouillon, 2 cups water, and the thyme and bring to a boil.

7. Reduce the heat to a simmer, carefully slide the chicken breasts into the simmering stock, and poach, uncovered, for 10 minutes. Use tongs to remove the chicken and transfer to a cutting board to cool.

8. Add the potato to the pot and simmer for 30 minutes.

9. Cut the cooled chicken breasts into a medium dice and return to the pot.

10. Add the mushrooms, zucchini, and arugula and simmer for 15 minutes, allowing the flavors to meld and the arugula to wilt.

11. Add the peas and vinegar and let the peas warm through, about 5 minutes.

12. Season to taste with salt and pepper and serve.

PEGGY'S CHILI

SERVES 6 • **PREP TIME:** 20 minutes • **COOK TIME:** 2½ hours • **TOTAL TIME:** 3 hours

In the summer of 1986, my siblings and our families took a vacation on Martha's Vineyard and stayed at Dan Aykroyd's house, which was large enough to hold twenty-six Murrays. This was the same year that the movie *One Crazy Summer* came out, and my brother Joel was in it. Part of the movie was shot nearby, on Nantucket. Every time Johnny and I saw someone with a

Laura, Billy, and Brian

New England Patriots' shirt on, we would laugh at them because this was the summer after the Chicago Bears had trounced the Patriots in the Super Bowl.

One day when I needed a break from making meals, I said to Peggy, "Please do the cooking." Peggy obliged and made chili—and to this day, it's one of the best chilis I've ever had. This was the first time I'd ever had chili without ground beef, and you'll see that what makes this recipe stand out is the beef chuck.

2 tablespoons vegetable oil

2 to 2½ pounds beef chuck, cut into 2-inch cubes

1 large yellow onion, chopped

2 garlic cloves, minced

One 4-ounce can green chiles

One 10-ounce can beef consommé (not stock)

4 tablespoons tomato paste

2 teaspoons ground cumin

1 teaspoon dried oregano

One 16-ounce can kidney beans, rinsed and drained

1 to 3 teaspoons chili powder, depending on your heat preference

Kosher salt and freshly ground black pepper

continued

1. In a large Dutch oven over medium heat, heat the vegetable oil. Working in batches, add the cubed beef to the pot and brown on all sides, about 5 minutes per batch. Use a slotted spoon to transfer the beef to a plate and set aside.

2. Add the onion and garlic and sauté until translucent, 5 to 7 minutes.

3. Stir in the green chiles, consommé, tomato paste, cumin, and oregano. Cook for 5 minutes, allowing the flavors to incorporate.

4. Add the beef to the pot. Cover with the lid and simmer for 1½ to 2 hours, until the meat is tender.

5. Add the kidney beans and chili powder.

6. Season with salt and pepper to taste and serve.

CHEF ANDY'S NOTE: *Instead of simmering on the stovetop, this chili can also be placed in the oven at 300°F for 2 hours. Just be sure to use an oven-safe pot.*

CHEF ANDY'S NOTE: *If onions make you cry, place the sliced onions in ice water until you need them. This seems to decrease the amount of tears. But drain them well before cooking.*

FRENCH ONION SOUP

SERVES 8 • **PREP TIME:** 15 minutes • **COOK TIME:** 1 hour 30 minutes • **TOTAL TIME:** 1 hour 45 minutes

French onion soup was served at Mortimer's on a regular basis, and at our Murray Bros. Caddyshack restaurants, it's served every Wednesday. It takes a lot of onions to make this soup great. Browning the cheese under the broiler creates a very elegant dish. I've also added some things since I first started preparing it, including chicken stock, which kicks up the flavor. When you have done it once, it'll become a staple. Trust me—I have customers who travel a long way for this soup every Wednesday.

4 tablespoons (½ stick) unsalted butter

5 large yellow onions, sliced vertically

1 teaspoon sugar

1 short French baguette, cut into ½-inch slices

2 sprigs fresh thyme

1 cup dry red wine

2 quarts beef stock

1 quart chicken stock

Kosher salt and freshly ground black pepper

8 ounces Swiss or Gruyère cheese, shredded (about 2 cups)

1. Preheat the oven to 350°F.

2. In a large Dutch oven over low heat, melt the butter. Add the onions and sauté, stirring frequently. After 20 minutes, stir in the sugar. Continue cooking and stirring until the onions caramelize, another 20 to 25 minutes.

3. Arrange the bread on a large baking sheet and toast in the oven for 5 to 10 minutes. Set aside on a cooling rack.

4. When the onions are browned, add the thyme and wine. Continue cooking, uncovered, until the wine is almost evaporated, about 5 minutes. Add both the beef and chicken stocks and simmer for 30 minutes over medium heat. Remove the thyme stems and discard. Season with salt and pepper to taste.

5. Preheat the oven broiler to high. Divide the cheese among the tops of the toasted bread and place under the broiler to melt and brown the cheese, about 3 minutes. (Keep an eye on this to avoid burning.)

6. Ladle the soup into 8 bowls, place 1 cheese toast on top, and serve.

CHEF ANDY'S NOTE: *I often serve with croutons or sautéed sliced sausage on top. If you want to get fancy with the sausage, kielbasa is the way to go.*

SPLIT PEA SOUP

SERVES 6 • **PREP TIME:** 15 minutes • **COOK TIME:** 1 hour 30 minutes • **TOTAL TIME:** 1 hour 45 minutes

This soup has gotten a bad rap because of *The Exorcist*, but I think it's delicious. I could eat this soup every day. Ham hocks are available at any grocery store or butcher. Be sure to rinse your peas, picking them over in the strainer to be sure there are no small pebbles. It doesn't happen often, but you just want to be sure!

2 tablespoons extra virgin olive oil

1 pound smoked ham hocks (about 2 ham hocks)

1 medium yellow onion, cut into medium dice

2 medium leeks, white and light green parts only, thinly sliced and well rinsed

4 garlic cloves, minced

Kosher salt and freshly ground black pepper

2 medium carrots, diced

1 pound dried split green peas

½ tablespoon chopped fresh thyme

1½ quarts chicken stock or water, plus more as needed

1. In a large Dutch oven over medium heat, heat the olive oil. Add the ham hocks and brown lightly, about 6 minutes.

2. Add the onion, leeks, and garlic and season generously with salt and pepper. Continue cooking until tender, 7 to 8 minutes.

3. Stir in the carrots, peas, and thyme. Pour in the chicken stock and bring to a boil, then reduce the heat and simmer, partly covered. Stir occasionally until the peas are tender, about 1 hour and 15 minutes.

4. Remove the ham hocks and set aside on a plate to cool.

5. Using an immersion blender, give the soup a couple of quick blitzes, 3 to 5 seconds each. Add more stock to thin if necessary. The texture will be semi-smooth.

6. If desired, trim some meat off the ham hocks and add it to the soup. Otherwise, discard the ham hocks.

7. Season with salt and pepper to taste and serve.

MORTIMER'S PISTOU SOUP

SERVES 8 • **PREP TIME:** 20 minutes • **COOK TIME:** 40 minutes • **TOTAL TIME:** 1 hour

Glenn, the owner of Mortimer's, was so rude *The New Yorker* referred to him as a "gruff, tough gatekeeper to society." The Zagat Survey described an experience at Mortimer's this way: "If you haven't been on Page Six lately, plan to sit by the coat rack." But one thing that was a nice distraction to being seated by the kitchen (or the coat rack) was the outstanding cuisine. Our pistou—a French vegetable soup that is rarely found in restaurants today—was very popular. I was told by my French friends that this was the go-to comfort soup made by their mothers whenever the kids weren't feeling well. It really feels gourmet with the pesto addition at the end. It was a staple at Mortimer's, but I've adjusted the recipe many times over the years—such as replacing veal stock with beef stock and cutting down on the amount of rosemary—to make it even *more* comforting.

2 tablespoons unsalted butter

1 medium yellow onion, cut into ¼-inch dice

4 celery stalks, cut into ¼-inch dice

3 medium carrots, cut into ¼-inch dice

⅔ cup petite French lentils

One 28-ounce can whole tomatoes, crushed, with their juice

Pinch of dried thyme

Pinch of dried rosemary

1 quart chicken stock

2 cups beef stock

1 tablespoon concentrated beef-base bouillon or 1 cube beef bouillon

4 large egg yolks

½ cup chopped fresh basil

2 ounces Parmesan cheese, grated (about ½ cup)

2 tablespoons minced garlic

½ cup olive oil

Kosher salt and freshly ground black pepper

1. In a large Dutch oven over low heat, melt the butter. Add the onion, celery, and carrots and sweat the vegetables, stirring frequently, for 5 to 7 minutes.

2. Add the lentils, tomatoes, thyme, and rosemary and stir in to mix.

3. Add both the chicken and beef stocks, 1 quart water, and the bouillon. Simmer uncovered until the lentils are cooked, 20 to 25 minutes. Remove from the heat.

4. In a medium bowl, whisk together the egg yolks, basil, Parmesan, and garlic. Slowly whisk in the olive oil.

5. Whisk a small amount of the hot soup into the egg mixture. Very slowly, and stirring constantly to avoid having scrambled eggs, add this egg mixture into the soup. Return to a simmer.

6. Season with salt and pepper to taste and serve.

BILLI BI SOUP

SERVES 4 • **PREP TIME:** 15 minutes • **COOK TIME:** 20 minutes • **TOTAL TIME:** 35 minutes

CHEF ANDY'S NOTE: *Finding cleaned, debearded mussels is quite simple, but they always need to be rinsed before using. Many fish counters in the grocery store carry them, but it's always best to find a good fishmonger. Frozen mussels don't taste the same.*

This recipe hails from France in the early 1900s when American industrialist William B. Leeds Sr. journeyed to Europe and was a frequent diner at Maxim's in Paris. He had their cream of mussel soup so often the dish eventually become known as Billi Bi over the years. This was a recipe that Craig Claiborne, a famous food writer in New York in the 1960s, called "the most elegant and delicious soup ever created." It's also one of the easiest soups to make. This was one of the regular soups on the Mortimer's menu. My version has less cream, and I use the mussel meat in the dish, which we never did at the restaurant. It's always a big hit for any dinner party. Just the name makes it seem really fancy, but it's simple and delicious.

2 pounds mussels, scrubbed and rinsed (see Chef Andy's Note)

2 shallots, coarsely chopped

2 small white onions, quartered

2 sprigs parsley

Pinch of cayenne pepper, plus more as needed

1½ cups dry white wine

2 tablespoons unsalted butter, cubed

1 bay leaf

2 sprigs fresh thyme

2 cups heavy cream

1 egg yolk, lightly beaten

Kosher salt and freshly ground black pepper

1. Place the mussels in a large Dutch oven and add the shallots, onions, parsley, cayenne, wine, butter, bay leaf, and thyme. Cover and bring to a medium boil over medium-high heat, 8 to 10 minutes, until the mussels open. Discard any that do not open.

2. Use tongs to pick out the 8 biggest and plumpest mussels, and set them aside (in their shells) in a small bowl.

3. Strain the cooking liquid through a colander or fine-mesh sieve into a small bowl and set aside. This will be the base for the soup. Discard the vegetables.

4. When cool enough to handle, remove the mussels that were set aside from their shells.

5. In a small saucepan over medium heat, bring the reserved cooking liquid to a low boil. Add the cream, increase the heat to medium-high, and return to a low boil. Remove the pan from the heat and let the soup cool slightly, about 5 minutes. Add the egg yolk, stirring vigorously.

6. Carefully season with salt and pepper to taste. Divide the soup among four bowls. Place the mussels on top of the soup in the bowls.

5

BETWEEN BREAD:

SANDWICH STAPLES

ALL YOU NEED IS A HANDFUL

Left to right: Joel, Johnny, Andy, Billy, Edward, and Brian

In the Murray family kitchen, you would likely find one of the brothers eating a sandwich over the sink. Mom hated messes, but worse than that, if you got a dish dirty, you'd have to clean it. We found the best way to avoid washing a dish was to just eat while standing up, and a sandwich was the easiest because it made fewer crumbs. Eating on the go is a trick we learned when we were kids while caddying to make a few extra bucks. This is also where I was introduced to "the halfway house," a place to grab a snack between the front and back 9.

Golf has always been a huge part of my life—and the lives of all six of the Murray brothers. As I mentioned earlier, my brother Edward won an Evans Scholarship. My next brother, Brian, was definitely drawing from his experiences as a golf caddy when he wrote *Caddyshack* in the late 1970s. (Fun fact: Danny Noonan in *Caddyshack* was competing for a caddy scholarship just like Edward's.) My brother Billy not only caddied for many years, but he also began running the halfway house on a course called Canal Shores in our town.

The halfway house is usually located between the 9th and 10th holes, where traditionally it serves hot dogs, basic sandwiches, and drinks so golfers (and caddies) can refuel for the back 9.

Losing a bet to Billy

When I was living in Los Angeles, I used to golf with my brothers Joel and Brian every Monday at Rancho Park Golf Course. As far as public courses go, this place was fabulous—let's just say we never had to look to find a fourth!

MURRAY IN A MINUTE: *Make most of the recipes in this chapter in less than 45 minutes.*

As with most sports enthusiasts, golfers are often superstitious. One time after grabbing a bite at the halfway house, we *really* started slumping. So Brian decided to blame the hot dogs.

"That's it!" he yelled. "I'm done with hot dogs. I'm switching to hard-boiled eggs." (Every halfway house seems to offer hard-boiled eggs.)

Henceforth, we ditched the hot dogs and traded them for hard-boiled eggs with shaved onions and hot sauce from the condiment tray. Believe it or not, our games greatly improved!

Halfway houses offer other foods too: Tuna salad, egg salad, and chicken salad are all standbys. But the best thing to have at a halfway house is grilled cheese. And let me tell you, my grilled pimento cheese sandwich is a game changer.

This chapter is a mix of new favorites, like Pulled Pork Sandwich (page 91) and Turkey-Artichoke Sandwich (page 94), and old classics, as you'll see with the Peanut Butter, Lettuce, and Mayo Sandwich (page 86) from my childhood. And every good Catholic boy has a tuna salad in his repertoire, so of course that's here too (see page 88).

Singing usually comes at the 19th hole.

GRILLED PIMENTO CHEESE SANDWICH

SERVES 8 • **PREP TIME:** 20 minutes • **COOK TIME:** 30 minutes • **TOTAL TIME:** 50 minutes

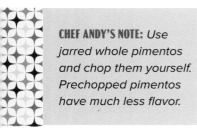

CHEF ANDY'S NOTE: *Use jarred whole pimentos and chop them yourself. Prechopped pimentos have much less flavor.*

I have to give my friend Martha Walters credit for inspiring this recipe. Her husband is one of Billy's best friends, and she makes the most incredible sandwiches. High-quality bread will help your sandwich really stand out. Here is one of her specialties.

8 ounces sharp yellow Cheddar cheese, shredded (about 2 cups)

8 ounces sharp white Cheddar cheese, shredded (about 2 cups)

4 ounces cream cheese, softened

One 4-ounce jar pimentos, well drained and finely chopped (see Chef Andy's Note)

3 tablespoons mayonnaise

1 tablespoon finely grated yellow onion

Pinch of cayenne pepper

16 slices of your favorite bread (I like sourdough)

4 tablespoons unsalted butter, melted

1. Place both Cheddars, the cream cheese, pimentos, mayo, grated onion, and cayenne in a large bowl and hand-mix to combine well. (Alternatively, place the ingredients in the bowl of a stand mixer fitted with the paddle attachment and mix on a slow speed for 2 minutes.)

2. Spread the mixture equally on 8 slices of the bread and top each with a second slice. Brush melted butter on the top and bottom sides.

3. Working in batches, place 2 sandwiches in a large skillet over medium heat and cook until melted on the inside and golden brown on the outside, 3 to 4 minutes on each side.

PEANUT BUTTER, LETTUCE, AND MAYO SANDWICH

SERVES 1 · **PREP TIME:** 5 minutes · **ASSEMBLY TIME:** 3 minutes · **TOTAL TIME:** 8 minutes

One April Fool's Day, Mom got up early and used some of the hard-boiled eggs from Easter to make our lunches. I can remember being surprised when I opened my lunch and found my usual peanut butter, lettuce, and mayo sandwich replaced by a hard-boiled egg—still in the shell!—between the bread. She definitely got the last laugh with that one.

To this day, most of my siblings still make this sandwich as a snack. And, out of habit, I'll still sometimes eat it over the sink! Here's the PB, L, and M sandwich.

1 to 2 tablespoons extra-crunchy Skippy peanut butter

2 slices white sandwich bread

1 tablespoon Hellmann's mayonnaise

Handful of iceberg lettuce leaves

1. Spread the peanut butter on 1 slice of the bread. Spread the mayo on the other slice.

2. Place the lettuce on top of the peanut butter and top with the mayo slice. Cut in half and eat over the sink if you're worried about crumbs.

TUNA SALAD SANDWICH

SERVES 4 • **PREP TIME:** 10 minutes • **ASSEMBLY TIME:** 5 minutes
TOTAL TIME: 45 minutes (includes refrigeration time)

Brian, Jay, Peggy, Ed, Lucille, Nancy, and Billy at Peggy and Jay's wedding

Peggy retelling the Jell-O story in front of her tuna and Jell-O–shaped cakes at her and Jay's fiftieth wedding anniversary party

When my sister Peggy started dating her now-husband, Jay, Mom always made ham and au gratin potatoes. It was her go-to for when company was coming to dinner. After a few times, Peggy asked if we could have something different.

"What does he like to eat?" Mom asked.

"Well, I know he likes tuna," Peggy said.

When Mom brought dinner to the table, she was so proud. But we kids were horrified. She had put the tuna *inside* a green Jell-O mold . . . with the Jell-O. And when that tuna/Jell-O combo was passed around the table, nobody would touch it. The plate came all the way back around to Mom. But Jay was such a trouper, he ate more than one serving.

While that dish might not have been a keeper, Jay certainly was. Here's my take on a classic tuna sandwich (minus the Jell-O).

continued

Two 5-ounce cans white albacore tuna, packed in water, drained well

Juice of ½ lemon

1 hard-boiled egg, peeled

2 tablespoons sweet pickle relish

2 tablespoons finely chopped celery

1 tablespoon minced scallions

⅓ cup mayonnaise

Kosher salt and freshly ground black pepper

8 slices sandwich bread, toasted

1. In a small bowl, break up the tuna with a fork. Add the lemon juice.

2. Grate the egg into the tuna. (I use a box grater.)

3. Add the relish, celery, scallions, mayo, and salt and pepper and mix to combine. Taste for seasoning and adjust as desired.

4. Cover and refrigerate for at least 30 minutes.

5. Spread the tuna salad equally on 4 slices of the toasted bread, covering each with a second slice.

PULLED PORK SANDWICH

SERVES 8 TO 10 · **PREP TIME:** 20 minutes · **COOK TIME:** 3 hours 30 minutes
TOTAL TIME: 4 hours (includes resting times)

This sandwich is a perfect dish for watching any sporting event. There's something about eating pulled pork while cheering for your favorite team that just seems like a fit. If you make too big of a batch, you can freeze the pork (it keeps for up to 6 weeks) since it reheats really well—perfect for a snack pretty much anytime!

3 tablespoons brown sugar

1 tablespoon smoked paprika

1 teaspoon garlic powder

1 teaspoon onion powder

1 teaspoon ground cumin

1 tablespoon kosher salt

½ tablespoon freshly ground black pepper

3- to 4-pound pork butt

2 tablespoons vegetable oil

One 12-ounce can beer of your choice

1 cup apple cider

8 to 10 buns, for serving

BBQ SAUCE

1½ cups ketchup

⅓ cup apple cider vinegar

½ cup Dijon mustard

¼ cup packed dark brown sugar

2 tablespoons Worcestershire sauce

1. In a small bowl, combine the brown sugar, paprika, garlic powder, onion powder, cumin, salt, and pepper. Rub the spice mixture into the pork. Let sit for at least 1 hour to allow the pork to absorb the spices.

2. Preheat the oven to 300°F.

3. Trim the excess fat from the pork.

4. In a large Dutch oven over medium-high heat, heat the oil. Add the pork and sear on all sides, about 15 minutes total. The sugar can burn quickly, so don't let it go too long.

continued

5. Pour the beer and apple cider around the pork and cover. Transfer to the oven and cook for about 3 hours. Remove the lid and cook for another hour, or until the meat is tender.

6. Transfer the pork to a plate to rest, about 10 minutes.

7. Make the BBQ sauce: Leave about 1 tablespoon of fat drippings in the Dutch oven, discarding the rest. Whisk in the ketchup, vinegar, mustard, brown sugar, and Worcestershire sauce and bring to a boil. Reduce the heat and simmer until the sauce thickens slightly, about 5 minutes. Remove from the heat and cover.

8. Place the pork in a large bowl and use two forks to shred the meat.

9. Toss the meat with half of the BBQ sauce. Add a little more sauce if needed. Divide the mixture among the buns, serving with the remaining sauce on the side.

Murray Bros. Caddyshack restaurant in St. Augustine, Florida

CHEF ANDY'S NOTE: *If you have a favorite coleslaw, this is a great opportunity to pile some on top of your pork sandwich.*

TURKEY-ARTICHOKE SANDWICH

SERVES 8 • **PREP TIME:** 15 minutes • **COOK TIME:** 40 minutes • **TOTAL TIME:** 1 hour 5 minutes

CHEF ANDY'S NOTE:
Precooked roasted chicken (white or dark meat) is a good substitute for the turkey breast.

This is another one of Martha Walter's specialties. She had a grilled cheese food truck, and it was so successful that somebody offered her a ton of money to buy her out. It wasn't me, if you were wondering—but I get it! Every year she and her husband have a party the day after Christmas, where she makes mini grilled cheese sandwiches. I went nuts over them. Here is an inspired version of her turkey-artichoke sandwich.

1½ pounds cooked turkey breast

1 cup mayonnaise

1 pound Parmesan cheese, grated (about 4 cups)

1 teaspoon ground white pepper, or ½ teaspoon freshly ground black pepper

Two 14-ounce cans artichoke hearts, drained and chopped

4 ounces Pepper Jack cheese, shredded (about 1 cup)

16 slices sourdough bread

4 tablespoons (½ stick) unsalted butter, melted

1. Place the turkey in a large bowl and use two forks to shred the meat.

2. In another large bowl, mix together the mayo, Parmesan, and pepper. Stir in the artichokes and Pepper Jack cheese. Add the turkey and mix well to combine.

3. Spread the mixture evenly on 8 bread slices, then top each with the remaining slices.

4. Brush the tops and bottoms of all the sandwiches with melted butter.

5. Working in batches, place 2 sandwiches in a large skillet over medium heat and cook until golden brown, about 5 minutes per side.

6

THE
MAIN EVENT:
MEAT

NO ELBOWS ON THE TABLE

Our corner grocery store, Pearson's, was a small family-run place with high-quality meats. They had three full-time butchers, and it was my job to pick up whatever was needed. I never minded, because they sold these little chocolate shakes—like a half-pint. I would get one of those as my reward for going to the store. When you were ten years old, that was a pretty great reward—and probably still would be now.

Like I mentioned earlier, my dad was a meat-and-potatoes guy. There was a theory back then that meat was better for his diet than anything else, so on Fridays, when the rest of us would be having some sort of tuna noodle casserole, my dad would occasionally go over to his mother's house and she would make him a steak. His favorite meal was a simple bone-in, standing rib pork roast, which is a beautiful cut of meat. And my father could carve! When my parents got engaged, my mother took a cooking class and my father took a carving class.

Dad getting ready to carve

I'm grateful that I had so many family dinners growing up, and I think more people are appreciating the importance of the family gathering at the table, complete with some table manners and plenty of good stories. Every dinner at our dining room table, Sunday through Thursday, was a sit-down meal with the whole family. We always had a stack of bread, with butter, placed on the table.

I sat to my father's left, so I was the last person to be served. Dad liked his meat well done—there was no pink to be found. You had to eat fast because if you didn't, your siblings would take your food right off your plate. (I had some pretty quick fingers myself!)

I tried to be a vegetarian when I was at Second City. I was on the stage and I had no energy. Harold Ramis, who was one of my closest friends, looked at me and said, "You're so lethargic on stage. You need to go eat a burger or something!" So I started eating meat again. My vegetarian phase lasted about a week.

—BRIAN

As we got older, and after Dad passed away, friends would get invited to join the Murray family for a sit-down dinner. And even after we were all grown up, whenever one of us (or our friends) needed a "Lucille fix," they would come back to Wilmette and be welcomed with good food and great hospitality. I'll never forget the time Brian invited John Belushi over for fried chicken when they were at the Second City together. (More on that soon . . .)

One thing the pandemic has done for many is to "bring back the family meal" at the table, not in front of the television. While I still feel nostalgic remembering my dad slowly carving the meat, I sometimes wonder what he would think of how my palate has changed over the years. The many stages I've passed through in my cooking history have definitely expanded my horizons. There are a lot of ways to use meat in the main course. Here are some of my favorites.

PORK ROAST, MURRAY-STYLE

SERVES 8 TO 10 • **PREP TIME:** 35 minutes • **COOK TIME:** 1 hour 30 minutes
TOTAL TIME: 2 hours 15 minutes (includes resting times)

This is a special-occasion meal. You can buy a pork roast that is deboned, but it won't be as flavorful as bone-in, and the presentation won't be as impressive. This recipe showcases how Lucille would make the pork roast "Murray-style" (but unlike my dad, I do prefer a little pink in the middle).

1 tablespoon kosher salt

1 teaspoon freshly ground black pepper

2 teaspoons garlic powder

1 teaspoon chopped fresh thyme

2 tablespoons olive oil

4- to 5-pound center-cut pork roast, with ribs and fat cap (ask your butcher to leave the fat cap on)

1. Preheat the oven to 400°F.

2. In a small bowl, mix together the salt, pepper, garlic powder, and thyme.

3. Rub the oil all over the meat, then liberally rub the seasonings into it. Let it sit for 30 minutes before cooking.

4. Place the pork in a roasting pan and roast for 90 minutes, until the internal temperature reads 155°F. Transfer the pork to a cutting board and let rest for 10 minutes before carving. Slice and serve.

JAMBALAYA

SERVES 8 TO 12 • **PREP TIME:** 30 minutes • **COOK TIME:** 1 hour 30 minutes • **TOTAL TIME:** 2 hours

Around 1983–84, Cajun restaurants were opening all over New York. That's when I had my first taste of New Orleans–style cooking. Pete Thompson was one of my kitchen managers at Murray Bros. Caddyshack, and his ex-wife had the best recipe for jambalaya. People who came to our restaurant just raved about it. I made a couple of tweaks, and here is what Murray Bros. proudly serves.

4 tablespoons (½ stick) unsalted butter

1½ pounds andouille sausage, sliced into ¼-inch rounds

1½ pounds chicken thighs, cut into ½-inch dice

1 pound ham, cut into ½-inch dice

1½ cups chopped onions

1 cup chopped celery

1½ cups chopped green bell pepper

2 tablespoons finely chopped garlic

One 28-ounce can crushed tomatoes

4 cups chicken stock

1 bay leaf

1 teaspoon gumbo filé or filé powder

1 teaspoon cayenne pepper

1 teaspoon dry mustard

1 teaspoon ground white pepper

½ teaspoon ground cumin

½ teaspoon dried thyme

1 teaspoon kosher salt

½ teaspoon freshly ground black pepper

2 cups uncooked white rice

1½ pounds shrimp, peeled, deveined, and tails off

1. In a large Dutch oven over medium heat, melt the butter. Add the sausage, chicken thighs, and ham and sauté for 10 minutes, turning when the meat has browned.

2. Add the onions, celery, bell pepper, and garlic and cook until the onions are translucent, 12 to 15 minutes.

3. Add the tomatoes, chicken stock, bay leaf, gumbo filé, cayenne, dry mustard, white pepper, cumin, thyme, salt, and black pepper and cook over low heat, simmering for about 1 hour.

CHEF ANDY'S NOTE: *Don't swap out chicken thighs for breasts—the breasts will be overcooked. And don't mess with the spices!*

4. Stir in the rice and continue simmering uncovered until the rice is tender, about 20 minutes.

5. Add the shrimp and stir until opaque, about 2 minutes.

6. Fish out the bay leaf and discard. Divide the jambayala evenly among bowls and serve hot.

RACK OF LAMB

SERVES 2 TO 4 • **PREP TIME:** 10 minutes • **COOK TIME:** 20 to 30 minutes
TOTAL TIME: 45 minutes (includes resting time)

One night at Mortimer's there was a big party for Princess Margaret, sister of Queen Elizabeth. We were serving rack of lamb because that was our signature dish—it was cooked medium rare, and it always came out perfectly.

In the kitchen at **Mortimer's, circa 1988**

I remember looking into the dining room from the kitchen and seeing Margaret sitting in the back of the room, chain smoking. She put down her cigarette only to eat. We brought out the lamb to her table, and she called over the waiter and said, "I need you to cook this *very* well done." So he took it back to the kitchen and we cooked the hell out of it (even though it broke my heart). She ate it all. You can do that if you want, but at least try it medium rare first.

½ cup panko bread crumbs

1 ounce Parmesan cheese, grated (about ¼ cup)

1 tablespoon chopped fresh parsley

1 teaspoon minced garlic

1 tablespoon olive oil

Kosher salt and freshly ground black pepper

One (8- or 9-rib) rack of lamb

1 tablespoon Dijon mustard

continued

CHEF ANDY'S NOTE: *A full rack can be split in half to fit more easily in the pan, which will decrease cooking time by a few minutes.*

1. Preheat the oven to 425°F.

2. In a small bowl, mix together the bread crumbs, Parmesan, parsley, garlic, and olive oil. Set aside.

3. Place a large oven-safe frying pan on the stovetop over high heat.

4. Generously salt and pepper the lamb. Place the rack fat side down in the hot frying pan (no need to add butter or oil). Sear the meat for 4 to 5 minutes on one side. Remove from the heat. Flip the rack over, bone side up, and transfer the lamb to a cutting board.

5. Spoon the mustard on the back side of the browned lamb. With firm pressure, press the bread crumbs into the mustard. Return the lamb to the frying pan and place in the oven on the middle rack.

6. Cook for 20 to 30 minutes, until a meat thermometer reads 120°F. Remove the rack from the oven, transfer it to a serving plate, and loosely cover in foil. Allow the lamb to rest for 10 minutes before serving.

BILL BLASS MEAT LOAF

SERVES 8 • **PREP TIME:** 25 minutes • **COOK TIME:** 50 to 60 minutes
TOTAL TIME: 1 hour 30 minutes (includes resting time)

When my brother Brian was in New Preston, Connecticut, he lived down the road from famed designer Bill Blass. Mr. Blass, as we all called him, was also a dear friend of Glenn's (the owner of Mortimer's), and one time after Glenn came back from visiting Bill he said, "I had the most fantastic meat loaf!" The chili sauce makes a huge difference, keeping the meat moist. We got the recipe from Mr. Blass and made a few changes to make it our own. I've also added more things over the years, but I think he would approve.

CHEF ANDY'S NOTE: *Do not overmix the ingredients. Less handling will result in a more tender loaf.*

3 tablespoons unsalted butter

1 medium yellow onion, cut into ¼-inch dice

1 cup chopped celery

1 pound ground beef

1 pound ground veal

1 pound ground pork

1 bottle Heinz chili sauce

½ cup chopped fresh parsley

½ cup soft bread crumbs

2 tablespoons Worcestershire sauce

2 large eggs

1 tablespoon kosher salt

1 teaspoon freshly ground black pepper

1 cup ketchup

¾ pound bacon, sliced

1. Preheat the oven to 350°F.

2. Line a roasting pan with parchment paper.

3. In a large skillet over medium heat, melt the butter. Add the onion and celery and cook until the vegetables have softened, about 5 minutes. Transfer to a large bowl or to the bowl of a stand mixer fitted with the paddle attachment.

continued

4. Add the beef, veal, pork, chili sauce, parsley, bread crumbs, Worcestershire sauce, eggs, salt, and pepper. With clean hands, gently mix just enough to incorporate all the ingredients. Do not overmix. If using a stand mixer, mix on low speed for 1 minute.

5. Place the mixture on a sheet pan. Pat it into the shape of a Quonset hut, which looks like a half barrel with tapered ends.

6. Use a rubber spatula to spread the ketchup over the outside of the meat loaf, like icing. Arrange the bacon slices over the top of the loaf.

7. Bake for 50 minutes. If the bacon is not browned on top, bake for another 10 minutes. Let it rest for 10 minutes before serving.

LUCILLE'S FRIED CHICKEN

SERVES 2 TO 4 • **PREP TIME:** 15 minutes • **COOK TIME:** 40 minutes • **TOTAL TIME:** 55 minutes

When Brian started at the Second City and made it to the main stage, he shared that stage with people like Harold Ramis, Betty Thomas, John Belushi, and Joe Flaherty. One night, Brian brought John, Harold, and Joe to dinner over at our house.

Dinner at our house was always a show. This time was no different. My mom used a cast-iron pan with Crisco to fry chicken. Belushi must have eaten three chickens that night. He never came up for air. And the guys all loved my mother—they were gracious and funny. I thought I'd seen it all at our house, but that was a really special meal.

And I always laugh when I think of Belushi saying, "Bring me four fried chickens and a Coke," in *The Blues Brothers*, because I know for a fact he really did love a good fried chicken.

½ cup all-purpose flour

1 tablespoon sweet paprika

1½ teaspoons kosher salt

½ teaspoon freshly ground black pepper

3 to 3½ pounds bone-in, skin-on chicken, separated into parts

1 cup vegetable oil

1. In a large shallow dish or a paper bag, mix the flour, paprika, salt, and pepper. Coat the chicken with the flour mixture, either by rolling the pieces in the dish or shaking them in the bag.

2. In a large skillet with a lid, heat the oil over medium-high heat. Working in batches, carefully place the chicken pieces in the skillet skin side down. Do not overcrowd the pan. Cover and fry for about 10 minutes, until light brown.

3. Use tongs to turn the chicken pieces skin side up. Allow to fry, uncovered and undisturbed, for about 10 minutes, until the juice of the chicken runs clear. The chicken is cooked when a meat thermometer reads 165°F.

CHEF ANDY'S NOTE: *Flipping the chicken, then continuing to cook it uncovered helps keep the meat crispy. But the spattering oil can make a mess. To make cleanup easier, before I begin cooking, I'll sometimes line the stovetop with foil to catch the oil.*

JOHNNY'S MURRAY MEMORY

While Belushi was filming *The Blues Brothers*, he and Dan Aykroyd owned a little bar down the alley behind the Second City, so while they were shooting the movie, that was their personal hangout. One night Andy, Laura, and I were trying to convince my mom to stop by. I was really excited to go to a bar, and it was during the shooting of the movie, so Belushi and Aykroyd would be there.

We went up to the door, and there was this huge security guard who wouldn't let us in. Then my mom stepped up, clutching her purse, and said to this incredibly intimidating guard, "Will you please tell John that Mrs. Murray is here?"

The guy reluctantly went inside, and it wasn't two minutes later that Belushi came to the door and "Mrs. Murray" got carte blanche. John fawned all over my mother for forty-five minutes. Andy and I had two or three drinks, and then it was time to go. (My mom's drink of choice was usually an old-fashioned or maybe a Manhattan.)

Brian (*far right*) and John Belushi (*center in the glasses*)
with the cast of the Second City, 1971

CHICKEN POT PIE

SERVES 6 • **PREP TIME:** 30 minutes • **COOK TIME:** 1 hour 35 minutes • **TOTAL TIME:** 2 hours 5 minutes

The high-society women who frequented Mortimer's were very loyal and came in on a regular basis. The restaurant was their version of the corner saloon. And there was a certain pecking order in the way the tables were set up. Jackie Onassis and Brooke Astor always had to have the best seats.

These ladies had luncheon parties all the time, and their favorite dish was our chicken pot pie (with a country salad on the side). The crust wasn't too heavy, and the sauce was just right. It could be hard to please these women, but this recipe never disappointed. My version has more vegetables—such as celery and onions (Glenn would never allow onions or celery in the pot pie)—but I think those additions make it more like home.

2 tablespoons olive oil

4 skinless, boneless chicken breast halves (4 to 6 ounces each)

8 tablespoons (1 stick) unsalted butter

1 cup frozen pearl onions

3 medium carrots, cut into ½-inch dice

1 celery stalk, cut into ½-inch dice

8 ounces white button mushrooms, cleaned and sliced

½ cup all-purpose flour

1 quart chicken stock

1½ cups heavy cream

¼ cup dry vermouth

1 tablespoon chopped fresh thyme

1 tablespoon chopped fresh parsley

Kosher salt and freshly ground black pepper

1 sheet of frozen puff pastry, thawed

1 large egg yolk beaten with 2 teaspoons water

1. Preheat the oven to 425°F. In a large skillet over medium heat, heat the oil. Place the chicken in the skillet and cook until lightly browned, but not cooked all the way through, about 2 minutes on each side. Remove from the heat and allow the chicken to cool for about 10 minutes.

2. Cut the chicken into ½-inch cubes and place them in a large bowl.

3. In the same pan, melt 2 tablespoons of the butter and sauté the onions until translucent, 5 to 7 minutes. Transfer to the same bowl as the chicken.

continued

CHEF ANDY'S NOTE:
Shredding a precooked rotisserie chicken makes this dish easier.

4. Melt another 2 tablespoons of the butter and sauté the carrots, celery, and mushrooms until very lightly browned, 5 to 7 minutes. Transfer to the bowl with the chicken and onions. Mix, then set aside.

5. Melt the remaining 4 tablespoons butter over medium heat. Whisk in the flour and cook until lightly browned, 5 to 7 minutes. Slowly whisk in the chicken stock until smooth. Add the heavy cream, vermouth, thyme, and parsley. Season to taste with salt and pepper. Bring to a slow boil, then reduce the heat and simmer for 5 to 10 minutes, until the mixture is thick enough to coat the back of a spoon.

6. Pour the mixture into a 2-quart baking dish and evenly distribute the chicken and vegetables on top.

7. Roll out the pastry, ½ inch bigger than your baking dish. Cover the chicken and vegetables with the puff pastry and brush the pastry with the egg wash. Cut three 2-inch slits into the pastry for venting steam. Cook for 25 minutes, then turn the heat down to 350°F and cook for another 25 minutes, until the puff pastry rises and is a nice golden color and the sauce is bubbling.

SHORT RIBS WITH POLENTA

SERVES 4 • **PREP TIME:** 30 minutes • **COOK TIME:** 3 hours 30 minutes • **TOTAL TIME:** 4 hours

I first fell in love with short ribs when I went to Lucques, which was the "hot" restaurant in Los Angeles for a long time. Chef Suzanne Goin was just phenomenal. Since I was coming from New York, there weren't any restaurants that jumped out at me in L.A. until I went to Lucques. Suzanne made these fantastic short ribs, and from then on, I was determined that I was going to make short ribs as good as Suzanne's. I was sad to hear that Lucques closed. The restaurant was open for more than twenty years. Here's my version of short ribs, which I've tweaked over the years. It might not be exactly what I had at Lucques, but I think it's pretty darn close.

2½ to 3 pounds bone-in short ribs

Kosher salt and freshly ground black pepper

2 tablespoons vegetable oil

3 medium carrots, chopped

2 celery stalks, chopped

1 large Spanish onion, chopped

2 garlic cloves, smashed

1 tablespoon tomato paste

1½ cups dry red wine

1½ cups beef stock

3 sprigs fresh thyme

1 bay leaf

FOR THE POLENTA

1 teaspoon kosher salt

1 cup coarsely ground cornmeal

3 tablespoons unsalted butter

2 ounces Parmesan cheese, grated (about ½ cup)

1. Preheat the oven to 300°F.

2. Liberally sprinkle all sides of the short ribs with salt and pepper.

3. In a large Dutch oven over medium heat, heat the oil. Working in batches, sear the short ribs on all sides until browned, 3 to 4 minutes on each side. Set aside on a plate.

continued

CHEF ANDY'S NOTE: *The meat will be so tender you can remove the bones before serving if you'd like.*

4. Add the carrots, celery, onion, and garlic to the pot and sprinkle with salt and pepper. Cook until lightly browned, 10 to 12 minutes.

5. Push the veggies to the side and add the tomato paste. Cook for about 1 minute, until the paste is very lightly carmelized. Add the wine and deglaze the pot, scraping and incorporating any brown bits from the bottom. Add the beef stock and bring to a simmer. Add the thyme and bay leaf and season with salt and pepper.

6. Nestle the short ribs in the pot and pour in any juices from the plate. Transfer to the oven and cook for 3 hours, or until fork-tender. Use tongs to remove the ribs from the braising liquid and set aside on a clean plate to cool.

7. Skim the fat off the top of the braising liquid and discard. Strain the liquid through a fine-mesh sieve into a small bowl and return to the pot. Bring to a simmer and cook until the liquid is reduced by half, 8 to 10 minutes. Taste for seasoning and add more salt and pepper if desired.

8. Meanwhile, make the polenta: Pour 4 cups water into a large pot with a lid, add the salt, and bring to a boil over high heat. Pour the cornmeal into the boiling water, whisking constantly to avoid lumps, about 3 minutes. Reduce the heat to low and simmer, whisking often until the polenta thickens, about 5 minutes.

9. Cover and cook for 30 minutes, whisking every 5 minutes or so. Don't let it stick to the bottom of the pot and burn. When it's too thick to whisk, stir with a wooden spoon. The polenta is done when the texture is thick and creamy. Turn off the heat and stir in the butter until it melts. Mix in the Parmesan, cover, and let stand for 5 minutes. Stir and taste for salt before transferring to a serving bowl.

10. Serve the short ribs over the polenta (see Chef Andy's Note).

7

THE
MAIN EVENT:
FISH

NOT JUST FOR FRIDAYS

My family didn't really eat fish unless it was on Friday—and then it was either fish sticks or tuna casserole (complete with Campbell's cream of mushroom soup, frozen peas, and fried onions on top). When my mom did make fish, it was never fresh because fresh fish was nearly impossible to get in the Chicago suburbs at that time. I never had a taste for fish—that is, until I moved to New York.

In 1978, Billy was pushing me to come out east to look at the Culinary Institute of New York. This was when he was on *Saturday Night Live*. I really wanted to visit, so the following year, I planned a trip. There was a couple,

Annie Potts and Billy in the greenroom at *SNL*

Eric and Kitty Pergeaux, who did the catering for *SNL*, and Eric was from Paris. He really knew what he was doing.

We got to talking in the *SNL* greenroom. I told Eric that I was planning to go to culinary school, and he responded in his very thick French accent, "Come work with me and I will teach you everything. I've got a restaurant on Shelter Island."

So Memorial Day weekend of 1979, I showed up at his restaurant, La Terrace, on Shelter Island off Long Island. I walk in the door and ask for Eric. The guy in the kitchen wasn't having it. He calls Eric, who drives five miles to the restaurant, and Eric has *no* recollection of our conversation at all. (This is the problem with making business deals over too many gin and tonics.) He was not expecting me and was pretty annoyed that I'd shown up. I didn't know what to do, but they let me stick around.

Shelter Island was full of fishermen who caught everything right there off the docks. When something is fresh, and prepared with the right ingredients, it's a game changer. And this began my deep love for French cuisine and seafood.

There was one time when Dover sole actually saved the meal. It was 1986 or '87, and Frank Sinatra was performing at Madison Square Garden. Red Buttons was throwing a dinner party after the concert at Mortimer's for 15 to 20 people in the back room. And we were ready with our famous rack of lamb. We stayed late for them—the show didn't get over until 11:00 P.M., so it was 11:30 when they started arriving.

We served the main dish, and all of a sudden Barbara Sinatra comes through the kitchen door and says, "Hi, I'm Barbara Sinatra, and my husband and I don't eat lamb." (I got a kick out of the fact that she felt she needed to introduce herself.) And I said, "Would you like fish instead?" And she said, "Fish would be wonderful." So I look at my fish guy—his name was John—and I said, "Two Dover soles." They were simply sautéed and finished off in a lemon–brown butter sauce. We sent them out to Frank and Barbara, hoping for the best.

We get through the dinner service, and as the coffee was being served, Sinatra came walking into the kitchen. And we're all just standing there thinking, *Oh man, what did we do?* We wait for a beat, hoping we're not in trouble, and he says, "Who made that fish?" I point to John. Sinatra slowly pulls out this wad of cash, gives John $100, and says, "That was a great piece of fish." Then he reaches back into his money clip and gives $50 to each and every person in the kitchen. We were stunned.

While I can't guarantee this chapter's recipes will get you a $100 tip, I do know they all hold a place in my heart, from my best friend Mac's Clams (page 132) to my cousin Cathy Collins's Birthday Salmon (page 124). Our famous Murray Bros. Caddyshack Carl's Crab Cakes (page 126) won't disappoint either. Freshness matters with all fish, so know your source (or your house will smell for days like mine did when I was a kid). You'll notice some French inspiration in the dishes too, thanks to those months I spent on Shelter Island.

FRANK SINATRA'S DOVER SOLE

SERVES 4 • **PREP TIME:** 5 to 10 minutes • **COOK TIME:** 10 to 15 minutes • **TOTAL TIME:** 25 minutes

Frank Sinatra so loved the sole we served him at Mortimer's that he grandly tipped the entire kitchen staff. Everyone who worked in the restaurant ran to the front door to watch him leave, and when he and his entourage walked out onto Lexington Avenue under the canopy, we all started cheering for him. "The Best Is Yet to Come" was one of his hit songs, but let me tell you—that phrase also applies to this Dover sole, which we proudly served to the "Chairman of the Board."

MURRAY IN A MINUTE:
Make this dish in less than 30 minutes.

½ cup all-purpose flour

1 teaspoon kosher salt

½ teaspoon freshly ground black pepper

4 Dover soles (about 6 ounces each), filleted (see Chef Andy's Note)

4 tablespoons extra virgin olive oil or clarified butter

4 tablespoons unsalted butter

½ tablespoon chopped fresh parsley

4 lemon wedges, for serving

1. In a medium bowl, mix together the flour, salt, and pepper. Lightly dust the fish with the flour mixture, shaking off any extra to create a thin coating.

2. In a large skillet over medium heat, heat 2 tablespoons of the oil, then carefully slide 2 of the fish fillets into the pan. Gently shake the pan as you cook to keep the fish from sticking. As soon as the fillets are a golden color, about 5 minutes, flip them. Cook until the other side is golden brown, just a couple more minutes. Transfer the fish to a plate and cover loosely with foil to keep warm.

3. Heat the remaining 2 tablespoons oil and repeat the process for the remaining 2 fillets. Transfer the fillets to the plate with the first batch of fish and cover with foil. Remove the skillet from the heat.

4. Wipe the oil out of the skillet with a paper towel. Melt the butter in the skillet over medium heat and let brown, 1 to 2 minutes. Do not let it burn. Stir in the parsley. Spoon this mixture onto the fish. Serve immediately with lemon wedges on the side.

CHEF ANDY'S NOTE: *If you can find a good fishmonger who cleans and de-bones the fish, that's great and will save you lots of time.*

CATHY COLLINS'S BIRTHDAY SALMON

SERVES 6 • **PREP TIME:** 20 minutes • **COOK TIME:** 27 minutes • **TOTAL TIME:** 47 minutes

My cousin Cathy

My cousin Kevin's wife, Cathy, was always posting pictures and recipes for delicious-looking dishes on Facebook. So one year for her birthday, we threw her a party where everyone made a different recipe based on what she had posted. There was this salmon dish with a sweet chili sauce that looked promising. So I tweaked it, served it for her birthday dinner, and it was a big hit.

Later, when we asked Cathy which recipe was *her* favorite to make, she said, "Oh, I never made *any* of them. I just posted the pictures." This salmon has become a staple at family parties, but Cathy hasn't posted a picture of another recipe since.

Cooking spray

17 fresh or canned pineapple rings

3-pound side of salmon, skin removed

Kosher salt and freshly ground black pepper

3 tablespoons butter, melted

3 tablespoons sweet chili sauce

2 tablespoons chopped fresh cilantro

2 garlic cloves, minced

2 teaspoons grated peeled fresh ginger

2 teaspoons sesame oil

½ teaspoon crushed red pepper flakes

Toasted sesame seeds, for garnish

Thinly sliced scallions, for garnish

Lime wedges, for serving

1. Preheat the oven to 350°F.

2. Line a large rimmed baking sheet with foil. Cover with cooking spray. Place the pineapple slices, evenly layered, in the center of the baking sheet.

3. Season both sides of the salmon with salt and black pepper. Place on top of the pineapple slices, pretty side up.

4. In a small bowl, whisk together the butter, chili sauce, cilantro, garlic, ginger, sesame oil, and red pepper flakes. Brush all over the salmon.

5. Bake the salmon on the center rack for about 25 minutes, until it reaches desired doneness.

6. Switch the oven to broil. Broil the salmon for 1 to 2 minutes, until it is slightly golden.

7. Garnish with sesame seeds and scallions. Serve with lime wedges.

CARL'S CRAB CAKES

SERVES 4 • **PREP TIME:** 20 minutes • **COOK TIME:** 6 to 8 minutes
TOTAL TIME: 1 hour 30 minutes (includes refrigeration time)

This dish is named after the character Carl Spackler, played by my brother Billy in the movie *Caddyshack*. There is a place called Indian Creek Country Club in Miami Beach that had a buffet on Friday nights that included clams, oysters, lobsters, stone crab, and this huge bowl of lump crab. I stuffed myself every time. It was gluttonous, but it was heaven.

Now, a lot of restaurants use more bread crumbs than crabmeat to make their crab cakes as a way to save on costs. I don't do that at our restaurants. You need to use high-quality lump crabmeat as the base. More crab and less filler—that is my motto. It's not a big moneymaker, but it keeps people coming back again and again. It's about quality, not quantity—although I guarantee you'll want more of this dish.

½ cup mayonnaise

1 large egg, beaten

1 tablespoon Dijon mustard

1 tablespoon minced scallions

1 tablespoon Worcestershire sauce

1 teaspoon Old Bay seasoning

1 teaspoon lemon zest

1 pound jumbo lump crabmeat

¾ cup panko bread crumbs

¼ cup canola oil

Lemon wedges, for serving

Tartar sauce, for serving

1. In a small bowl, whisk together the mayo, egg, mustard, scallions, Worcestershire sauce, Old Bay seasoning, and lemon zest.

2. In a medium bowl, pick over the crabmeat and discard any shells. Add the bread crumbs and very lightly toss with the crabmeat. Gently fold in the mayo mixture. Be sure not to overmix, as that will break up the crabmeat. Cover and refrigerate for 1 hour to firm up the mixture.

3. Scoop the crab mixture into ⅓-cup mounds. Lightly pat them into 8 patties, each about 1 inch thick.

4. In a large skillet over medium-high heat, heat the canola oil until shimmering and, working in batches, panfry the crab cakes until golden brown and heated through, about 3 minutes on each side. Cover the finished cakes loosely with foil.

5. Serve immediately with lemon wedges and tartar sauce.

MUSSELS MEUNIÈRE

SERVES 2 AS A DINNER OR 4 AS AN APPETIZER • **PREP TIME:** 15 minutes • **COOK TIME:** 7 to 10 minutes
TOTAL TIME: 25 minutes

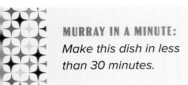

MURRAY IN A MINUTE:
Make this dish in less than 30 minutes.

This dish is a throwback to that 1979 summer working on Shelter Island. When mussels became one of the more popular items on the menu, I had to learn how to clean and debeard them rather quickly. We did each and every one by hand. Now, it's hard to find them *with* the beard—which makes them so much easier to prepare. I wish more people in my life liked mussels, because I would make them all the time. They are so simple, and the meat of a good mussel is incredibly satisfying. Here's one of my favorite mussel dishes.

3 tablespoons extra virgin olive oil

2 shallots, finely chopped

3 garlic cloves, finely chopped

2 pounds mussels, scrubbed and rinsed (see Chef Andy's Note on page 78)

1 cup dry white wine

1 cup heavy cream

2 tablespoons unsalted butter

¼ cup chopped fresh parsley

Pinch of kosher salt

Crusty bread, for serving

1. In a Dutch oven or a 6-quart pot with a lid, heat the olive oil over medium-high heat. Add the shallots and cook for 1 minute.

2. Add the garlic and cook, stirring, until fragrant, about 30 seconds, then add the mussels, wine, cream, butter, parsley, and salt. Stir and cover.

3. Cook until the mussels open, 7 to 10 minutes. Discard any mussels that haven't opened. Divide the mussels and juice between two bowls (or among four bowls, if an appetizer) and serve with bread.

SEA SCALLOPS WITH LEMON BUTTER

SERVES 2 • **PREP TIME:** 15 minutes • **COOK TIME:** 5 minutes • **TOTAL TIME:** 20 minutes

MURRAY IN A MINUTE:
Make this dish in less than 30 minutes.

My appreciation for scallops started after one of our Mortimer's customers brought in a bagful. They were diver scallops, and we ate them for two days straight. (They're called "diver" scallops because they're hand-caught by divers.) An unfortunate reality is there are some restaurants that have been known to pass off shark as scallops. They just use a small knife to shape the shark meat like a scallop. If you get a "scallop" that has no sweetness and smells a little fishy, it's probably shark.

The scallops I love the most are the Nantucket Bay scallops—they are sweeter and smaller. The problem is, they are very seasonal, which limits their availability; plus, they're expensive. You don't need Nantucket Bay scallops for this recipe, although I'd recommend giving them a try. Fresh garlic and some butter—that's all you need to make a great scallop.

1 tablespoon unsalted butter

1 tablespoon vegetable oil

1 pound large dry scallops

Kosher salt and freshly ground black pepper

LEMON-BUTTER SAUCE

2 tablespoons unsalted butter

2 garlic cloves, minced

Juice of 1 lemon

Kosher salt and freshly ground black pepper

2 tablespoons chopped fresh parsley

1. Remove any small side muscles from the scallops and discard. Rinse the scallops with cold water, then thoroughly pat dry.

2. In a large skillet over medium heat, melt the butter with the vegetable oil. Season the scallops with salt and pepper, then add to the skillet.

CHEF ANDY'S NOTE: *Do not overcook, or they will turn to rubber.*

3. Cook the scallops until they are golden brown, 3 to 4 minutes, then flip and cook for 1½ minutes more, or until the second side has turned golden brown. Remove the skillet from the heat. Transfer the scallops to a plate and cover loosely with foil to keep warm. Pour off any oil from the skillet.

4. Make the lemon-butter sauce: In the same skillet, melt the butter over medium-high heat. Add the garlic and cook until fragrant, stirring frequently, about 1 minute. Stir in the lemon juice and season to taste with salt and pepper.

5. Divide the scallops evenly between the two plates. Spoon the sauce over them, garnish with the parsley, and serve.

MAC'S CLAMS

SERVES 4 • **PREP TIME:** 5 minutes • **COOK TIME:** 7 to 10 minutes • **TOTAL TIME:** 15 minutes

Me and Mac

My business partner and one of my best friends is named Mac Haskell. He had a place on Martha's Vineyard, and we spent time there every year for decades. There are multiple fish markets on Martha's Vineyard, and they sell really high-quality clams. I always loved it when Mac made this dish. He would mix butter, wine, lemon, and a *lot* of chopped scallions. They are the key to this whole thing. If you don't have scallions, it just doesn't taste the same.

½ pound (2 sticks) unsalted butter

½ cup dry white wine

Juice of 2 lemons

Bunch of scallions, chopped

4 dozen littleneck or cherrystone clams, scrubbed

Crusty bread, for serving

1. In a medium saucepan with a lid over medium-high heat, melt the butter with the wine and lemon juice, then bring to a boil. Turn off the heat and whisk in the scallions. Cover to keep warm and set aside.

2. Fill a large pot with 1 quart water. Place the clams in a steamer attachment and lower them into the pot. Cover and steam over high heat. As soon as the clams open, they are done, 7 to 10 minutes. Discard any clams that haven't opened.

3. Divide the clams evenly among four bowls. Spoon the sauce into separate side bowls. Serve with crusty bread.

MURRAY IN A MINUTE:
Make this dish in less than 20 minutes.

8

TWIRLING FORKS: PASTA CLASSICS

THAT'S AMORE!

My parents were a dynamic duo, but at the dinner table, they had to divide and conquer, so they sat at opposite ends. With nine kids, there was plenty of policing that went on to make sure we all kept our elbows off the table and our napkins in our laps. While manners were a top priority during the meal, we also couldn't touch a bite until we said grace. Usually, it was led by Mom. Heads down, all together, we would recite, "Bless us, O Lord, for these, thy gifts, for which we are about to receive, from thy bounty, through Christ, our Lord. Amen." (Often, Mom would add an extra Hail Mary or two to cover our bases.)

Lucille and Edward Murray

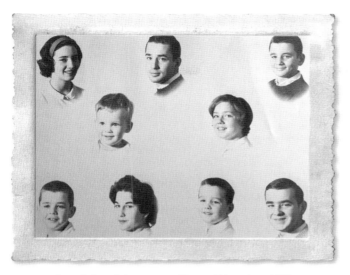

From left to right, top row: **Nancy, Edward, and Billy**
Middle row: **Joel and Laura**
Bottom row: **Me, Peggy, Johnny, and Brian**

But dinner at our house wasn't all manners and prayers. There were lots of laughs to be had. My parents were both quite funny, plus we had future comedic actors Brian, Billy, Johnny, and Joel in the bunch. And you can't discount Peggy's one-liners or Nancy's timing.

I mean, you just couldn't last in my family if you didn't have a good sense of humor. And it was a big deal if you could make my dad laugh.

When Dad died, the laughing stopped—for a while at least. It would eventually return to our family meals, but life as we knew it would never be the same. The emotional support that flooded in was incredible. Thankfully, we had neighbors, old friends, and, of course, family rise to the occasion to help us through. We knew we weren't alone.

After the funeral (the procession was like a mile long), everyone came back to our house, which could hardly hold all the people. There wasn't an inch in that house where you could move! Our Italian neighbors—the Zanzuccis, Ferrettis, Paolettis, DiClementis, and the Franchis— all swooped in and dropped off more food than I'd ever seen at one time. I couldn't believe it. We might have been grieving, but we were the best-fed family within a hundred-mile radius, that's for sure.

Mom in front of the Christmas tree

Ed and Lucille

When the house cleared out, the neighbor women took over our kitchen. I was amazed at how they handled the surplus of extra pasta. They had these seal machines—I'd never seen them before. They formed an assembly line and started sealing up all the food in bags and putting each bag in the freezer. All you had to do was throw it in hot water to reheat it for another meal. My mom had never made pasta. Not once. My dad didn't eat pasta, so *we* didn't eat pasta—but after that, I became a huge pasta fan.

This introduction to Italian cuisine sparked my culinary curiosity. I started making spaghetti with meat sauce whenever I could. For my thirteenth birthday (the age I am pictured at right) my mom let me have a sleepover where I cooked spaghetti for all my friends.

Clockwise from left to right: Peggy, Dad, Billy, Nancy, Mom, Brian, Edward, Laura, me, Johnny, and Joel. I was so proud of that red jacket—a gift for Christmas.

I will always be so grateful to our Italian neighbors for introducing me to the wonders of Italian food during a time when our world was crumbling around us. These families certainly brought comfort to our home that day—and for the weeks that followed. And I've been loving Italian food ever since.

The dishes in this chapter are great for family get-togethers. These are my favorite pastas—starting with Pasta Puttanesca (page 144), which I

Eighth grade graduation with Mom and my sister Nancy

PEGGY'S MURRAY MEMORY

At the end of saying grace, Mom would add a special intention. "Let's say a Hail Mary for so-and-so," she'd say, adding the name of someone who was sick or had died. But she would also add in something if she felt one of the kids was being negative. She would never name the child, but we would all know who it was. It could be "to help with our patience . . ." or "to learn to be a little kinder . . ." or "to help them get to bed earlier so they won't be as crabby." Some nights we prayed for Dale Long, a pitcher for the Chicago Cubs who lived on our street. But her favorite intention was "for our missing members." Whether one (or more) of us was away at school or just working a part-time job, Mom always prayed for all of us.

like better than any of the others. I could eat it every day if given the chance. But don't worry, meat lovers, the Lasagna with Italian Sausage (page 141) and Andy's Carbonara (page 146) have you covered. And except for the lasagna, every one of them can be made in 35 minutes or less!

Clockwise from top left: Johnny, me, Edward, Brian, Joel, Billy, Nancy, Mom, Laura, and Peggy

LASAGNA WITH ITALIAN SAUSAGE

SERVES 8 • **PREP TIME:** 30 minutes • **COOK TIME:** 2 hours 30 minutes
TOTAL TIME: 3 hours 15 minutes (includes resting time)

Anyone who lived through it remembers the blizzard of 1979. Chicago was hit with more than twenty inches of snow. During that time, my brother Johnny and I were working for a friend's father's trucking company. We quickly went from loading trucks to plowing the snow. There was a tiny Italian restaurant nearby with maybe ten tables, and basically, they catered to truckers. They made their Italian sausage from scratch, and it was unbelievable. I didn't realize just how good it was until I left Chicago. *Nobody* does Italian sausage like Chicago. Nobody (and I've been to a lot of places and eaten in a lot of restaurants). Fennel seeds in their sausage is what makes all the difference. To have a really good lasagna, you need to start with an authentic Italian sausage.

1 pound sweet Italian sausage links (about 5 links)

½ pound ground beef

½ cup finely chopped yellow onion

2 garlic cloves, crushed

¼ cup chopped fresh parsley

2 tablespoons sugar

1½ teaspoons dried basil

1½ teaspoons dried oregano

½ teaspoon fennel seeds

Kosher salt

¼ teaspoon freshly ground black pepper

Two 14-ounce cans whole tomatoes, undrained (about 4 cups)

Two 6-ounce cans tomato paste

12 curly-style lasagna noodles

15 ounces ricotta cheese, drained

1 large egg

12 ounces fresh mozzarella cheese, thinly sliced

2 ounces Parmesan cheese, grated (about ½ cup)

continued

1. Remove the sausage meat from the outer casings and chop as small as possible.

2. In a 5-quart Dutch oven over medium heat, sauté the sausage and beef, using a wooden spoon to break up the mixture. Add the onion and garlic and cook, stirring frequently, until well browned, about 20 minutes.

3. Add half of the parsley, the sugar, basil, oregano, fennel seeds, 1 tablespoon salt, and the pepper and mix well.

4. Add the tomatoes, tomato paste, and ½ cup water. Mash the tomatoes with a wooden spoon. Bring to a boil, then reduce the heat to a simmer. Cover and let simmer, stirring occasionally, until the sauce thickens, about 1½ hours.

5. In a large pot, bring 4 quarts water and 1 tablespoon salt to a boil. Add the lasagna, two noodles at a time to avoid sticking. Return to a boil, uncovered, stirring occasionally. Boil until tender, about 10 minutes. Use tongs or a spider to remove the lasagna noodles from the hot water, then rinse under cold water and pat dry with paper towels. Set aside on a plate.

6. Preheat the oven to 375°F.

7. In a medium bowl, combine the ricotta, egg, the remaining parsley, and ½ teaspoon salt. Mix well.

8. In a 9 × 13-inch baking dish, spread 1½ cups of the tomato-meat sauce evenly on the bottom of the baking dish. Layer with 4 lasagna noodles, lengthwise and overlapping, and spread a third of the ricotta mixture over the noodles. On top of that, arrange a third of the mozzarella slices. Repeat until the ingredients are gone. Sprinkle the Parmesan over the top.

9. Cover the baking dish with foil and bake for 25 minutes. Remove the foil, then bake for another 25 minutes, or until bubbly. Rest for 15 minutes before serving.

CHEF ANDY'S NOTE: *Don't mess with this recipe. You will be pleasantly surprised.*

PASTA PUTTANESCA

SERVES 4 TO 6 • **PREP TIME:** 15 minutes • **COOK TIME:** 17 minutes • **TOTAL TIME:** under 35 minutes

This is my favorite pasta dish—a savory delight that fills you up without making you feel like you've overdone it. Some people hate anchovies, but in this preparation, they melt into the sauce and add so much flavor. This is a fast dish, and impressive. You'll put this into your pasta rotation once you see how easy it is.

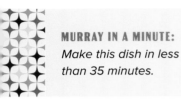

MURRAY IN A MINUTE:
Make this dish in less than 35 minutes.

¼ cup extra virgin olive oil

4 garlic cloves, finely chopped

4 anchovy fillets, chopped

One 28-ounce can whole tomatoes, crushed

½ cup pitted Kalamata olives

¼ cup drained capers

½ teaspoon crushed red pepper flakes

Kosher salt

1 pound spaghetti

Chopped fresh parsley, for garnish

1. In a large skillet over medium heat, heat the oil. Add the garlic and cook, stirring, until fragrant, about 1 minute.

2. Add the anchovies and cook until melting and fragrant, about another minute.

3. Add the tomatoes, olives, capers, and red pepper flakes. Bring to a boil, then reduce the heat and let simmer for 15 minutes. Season with salt to taste.

4. Bring a large pot of salted water to a boil, add the spaghetti, and cook according to the package directions, until al dente. Save ¼ cup of the cooking water for the sauce. Drain.

5. Add the reserved cooking water and the spaghetti to the sauce and simmer for 2 minutes.

6. Garnish with parsley and serve.

CHEF ANDY'S NOTE: *I've been known to swap out the pasta for two 15-ounce cans white cannellini beans (drained). It's a great alternative if you're cutting down on carbs.*

ANDY'S CARBONARA

SERVES 2 • **PREP TIME:** 15 minutes • **COOK TIME:** 15 to 20 minutes • **TOTAL TIME:** 30 to 35 minutes

This is basically an Italian version of bacon and eggs. And if I haven't mentioned it before, everything is better with bacon. It's such a simple dish, and you don't use cream, because the eggs mixed with the pasta water are enough. A big misconception about this dish is that it has butter and cream, but it's so flavorful already, you don't really need those ingredients.

Kosher salt

8 ounces bucatini or other long-noodled pasta

3 large eggs

2 ounces Parmesan, grated (about ½ cup), plus more for garnish

4 slices thick bacon, diced

4 garlic cloves, minced

Freshly ground black pepper

1 tablespoon chopped fresh parsley

1. Bring a large pot of salted water to a boil, add the bucatini, and cook according to the package directions, until al dente. Reserve ½ cup of the cooking water for the sauce, then drain the pasta and set aside.

2. In a small bowl, whisk together the eggs and Parmesan.

3. In a large skillet over medium-high heat, cook the bacon until browned, about 7 minutes. Add the garlic to the bacon and stir until fragrant, about 1 minute.

4. Reduce the heat to low. Working quickly, stir in the pasta and give it a toss. Add the egg mixture and toss again to mix. Add a little of the reserved pasta water until your desired consistency is reached.

5. Season to taste with salt and pepper. Garnish with the parsley and a little more Parmesan and serve.

SOUTH CAROLINA PAPPARDELLE

SERVES 4 • **PREP TIME:** 20 minutes • **COOK TIME:** 15 minutes • **TOTAL TIME:** 35 minutes

This is a dish that was inspired one night in Billy's South Carolina home. He had some people over and wanted me to "whip up" dinner. Burrata cheese had just come on the scene, so I experimented with it and some cherry tomatoes, and the combination was just perfect. The cheese just oozes out into the noodles, basil, and tomatoes. Throw in a glass of wine and some fresh bread, and you've got a perfect meal.

Kosher salt

1 pound pappardelle pasta

2 tablespoons extra virgin olive oil

Two 12-ounce containers cherry tomatoes

6 garlic cloves, thinly sliced

½ teaspoon freshly ground pepper

2 tablespoons unsalted butter

½ cup chopped arugula

1 teaspoon chopped fresh thyme

8 ounces burrata cheese (2 balls), balls cut in half (see Chef Andy's Note)

2 tablespoons chopped fresh basil, for garnish

Crushed red pepper flakes, for garnish

1. Bring a large pot of salted water to a boil, add the pappardelle pasta, and cook according to the package directions, until al dente. Reserve ¼ cup of the cooking water for the sauce, then drain the pasta and set aside.

2. In a large skillet over medium heat, heat the oil, then add the tomatoes and cook until blistered, about 3 minutes.

3. Reduce the heat to medium-low. Stir in the garlic, black pepper, and ¼ teaspoon salt. Cook until the tomatoes burst and start to collapse, about 10 minutes.

4. Add the cooked pasta, reserved pasta water, butter, arugula, thyme, and another ¼ teaspoon salt. Toss together very well.

5. Divide the pasta among 4 bowls. Top each with a halved burrata ball, then garnish with the basil and red pepper flakes.

CHEF ANDY'S NOTE: *Burrata comes in balls, so cut them in half before placing them on the pasta.*

PASTA WITH HARICOTS VERTS

SERVES 2 • **PREP TIME:** 15 minutes • **COOK TIME:** 15 minutes • **TOTAL TIME:** 30 minutes

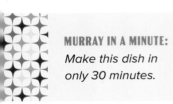

MURRAY IN A MINUTE:
Make this dish in only 30 minutes.

This recipe came to Mortimer's from famed chef, restaurateur, and author Alice Waters. She owns the acclaimed restaurant Chez Panisse in Berkeley, California, which is well known for initiating the farm-to-table movement. Some call her "the Mother of American Food." She sent one of her staff to show us a simple and impressive recipe, which I've since tweaked and made my own.

Kosher salt

2 ounces haricots verts, trimmed, cut into 1- to 1½-inch pieces (about ½ cup)

8 ounces spaghetti

½ cup olive oil

2 ounces sun-dried tomatoes, julienned (about ½ cup)

4 garlic cloves, minced

Freshly ground black pepper

1 tablespoon chopped fresh parsley

1. Bring a large pot of salted water to a boil, add the beans and spaghetti, and cook according to the package directions, until the spaghetti is al dente. When the pasta is done, drain both the beans and pasta.

2. In a large skillet over medium heat, heat the oil until shimmering. Add the tomatoes and garlic to the pan and remove from the heat. Let the tomatoes and garlic steep for at least 5 minutes to allow the flavors to infuse the oil.

3. Add the pasta and beans to the skillet and season to taste with salt and pepper. Toss vigorously for several minutes.

4. Divide the pasta between 2 bowls, garnish with the parsley, and serve.

CHEF ANDY'S NOTE: *The longer you steep the tomatoes and garlic in the oil, the more flavor and color will be infused.*

9

SAVE ROOM FOR DESSERT

SAVING THE BEST FOR LAST

Lucille blowing out the birthday candles

My mom loved sweets, but we didn't really keep any in the house when my dad was alive because he had diabetes. But after he passed away, there was always a carton of ice cream to be found in the freezer. There isn't a dessert that I don't like, and having more than one is fine with me. There's one time when dessert wasn't the only thing that was served twice. Let me tell you a story . . .

The movie *Caddyshack* was filmed in Davie, Florida, a town about thirty minutes outside of Fort Lauderdale. The budget for the movie was $6 million, which may sound small today, but at that time it was considered a decent amount of money. (To put it in context, another one of Billy's movies, *Meatballs*, was shot for about $1.2 million, and it brought in $70 million at the box office.)

While the producers had a decent budget for most things, money wasn't being spent on catering. The food on the set of *Caddyshack* was "mediocre at best," according to my brother Johnny.

"Some days they just laid out packages of bread with peanut butter," he said.

So one night, tired of the subpar cuisine, Billy got a group together to drive to Joe's Stone Crab in Miami. When you order at Joe's, it's quite a production. First they do a head count, and then you choose which size crab you want to eat. Billy ordered the large stone crabs, in addition to coleslaw, creamed spinach, sweet potato fries with honey, and of course, copious amounts of alcohol.

To finish it off, nothing other than key lime pie would do.

At the end of the meal, the server walked over to Billy.

"Can I get you anything else?" she asked.

Billy looked at her and said, "Yes, everything."

"What do you mean?"

"We want to order the whole meal again," Billy said.

And they did.

It wound up being a five-hour meal.

Now, I'm not saying that's the way things *should* be. What I'm saying is that while the key lime pie at Joe's is good, mine is better. The secret is the butter-rum glaze in between the graham cracker crust and the lime custard. I cover a lot of bases in this chapter—chocolate, cookies and ice cream, cheesecake, and Pineapple Upside-Down Cake (page 163), which I started tweaking when I was just twelve years old.

JOHNNY'S MURRAY MEMORY

After leaving Joe's Stone Crab, Billy and I cruised around Miami Beach, which was a bit seedy. Remember the motel scene from *Scarface*? At the time, Bill (and others) said he looked like Professor Irwin Corey, the malaprop comedian (who lived to be 102, by the way). Well, who do you suppose was leaning against a sandwich board advertising his show that night in front of the club? Professor Irwin Corey himself, smoking a joint between shows! He invited us into this burlesque house—which was so rundown the adobe tiles from the fake casita-style roof kept crashing down. Once the good professor finished his set, we called it a night.

KEY LIME PIE

MAKES ONE 9-INCH PIE • **PREP TIME:** 20 minutes • **COOK TIME:** 20 to 25 minutes
TOTAL TIME: 3 hours 45 minutes (includes cooling and refrigeration times)

This dessert has been on our restaurant menu in St. Augustine, Florida, since we opened in 2001. While it's had a few different variations, the key (pun intended) is the butter-rum sauce made with dark rum. As for the key lime juice, fresh key limes can sometimes be hard to come by, but Nellie and Joe's Famous Key West Lime Juice is widely available at any major grocery store. I use it every time, and so should you.

4 tablespoons (½ stick) unsalted butter

½ cup packed dark brown sugar

2 tablespoons dark rum

½ teaspoon kosher salt

One 9-inch graham cracker crust pie shell

4 large egg yolks

One 14-ounce can sweetened condensed milk

½ cup key lime juice

Zest from 1 lime

1. In a small saucepan over medium heat, melt the butter and sugar together, stirring, until the sugar dissolves, 5 to 8 minutes. Remove from the heat. Stir in the rum and salt. Set aside to cool for 10 minutes.

2. Scrape the butter mixture into the pie shell, evenly coating the bottom and sides.

3. Whisk together the egg yolks, sweetened condensed milk, key lime juice, and lime zest in a medium bowl. Pour the mixture evenly on top of the rum butter in the pie shell.

4. Bake at 325°F for 18 minutes. If the custard center jiggles when you tap the side of the pie, it's done. After baking, let the pie cool for at least 15 minutes, then refrigerate for 3 hours before serving.

HOMAGE TO ELVIS COOKIE

MAKES 6 COOKIES • **PREP TIME:** 20 minutes • **COOK TIME:** 10 to 15 minutes
TOTAL TIME: 1 hour 35 minutes (includes refrigeration time)

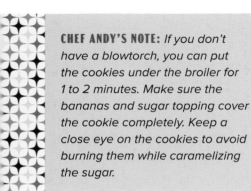

CHEF ANDY'S NOTE: *If you don't have a blowtorch, you can put the cookies under the broiler for 1 to 2 minutes. Make sure the bananas and sugar topping cover the cookie completely. Keep a close eye on the cookies to avoid burning them while caramelizing the sugar.*

I'm a huge Elvis fan. When I had the Andy Murray Band, there were a couple of Elvis songs I loved to do. And I knew all kinds of Elvis trivia, like the King was a *big* fan of peanut butter and banana sandwiches.

When I was working at the Tribeca Grill, the late, great Gerry Hayden made this dessert with a pecan cookie and bananas with malted milk ice cream on top. I figured, if you have bananas, why not honor Elvis and put some peanut butter in there—so I switched the pecan cookie for a peanut butter one.

This dessert, inspired by Gerry, is good enough to share, so you won't be "lonesome tonight." You can use whatever ice cream you'd like (pistachio is pictured here, but chocolate chip works well too).

2 sticks unsalted butter	1½ teaspoons baking powder
1 cup crunchy peanut butter	1 teaspoon baking soda
2 cups granulated sugar	½ teaspoon kosher salt
1 cup packed dark brown sugar	2 large ripe bananas
2 large eggs	1 quart your favorite ice cream
2½ cups all-purpose flour	

1. Preheat the oven to 375°F.

2. In the bowl of a stand mixer fitted with the paddle attachment, cream together the butter, peanut butter, 1 cup of the granulated sugar, and the brown sugar. Add the eggs, one at a time, on low speed until smooth.

continued

3. In a separate medium bowl, whisk together the flour, baking powder, baking soda, and salt. Add the dry ingredients to the wet and mix to combine on low speed.

4. Cover the dough and place in the refrigerator for 1 hour.

5. Roll the dough into 2-inch balls and put them on two baking sheets lined with parchment paper, 2 inches apart. Flatten each ball with a fork, making crisscross patterns on top.

6. Bake for 10 minutes, or until golden brown. Transfer to a wire rack to cool.

7. Transfer the cookies to a large plate. Slice the bananas into thin coins, layering them on each cookie and covering the cookies completely. Dust with the remaining granulated sugar and caramelize with a blowtorch, if available (see Chef Andy's Note).

8. To serve, place a cookie on a small plate and top with a scoop of your favorite ice cream. Serve immediately.

Singing with my band—probably belting out
Elvis's "Little Sister" or "Burning Love"

CHOCOLATE POTS DE CRÈME

SERVES 6 • **PREP TIME:** 40 minutes • **COOK TIME:** 10 minutes
TOTAL TIME: 3 hours 20 minutes (includes cooling and refrigeration times)

When I worked at a restaurant called West Broadway in New York, there was an incredibly talented pastry chef who made a pot de crème (which is just another version of chocolate pudding) that was to die for. Then I went up to Martha's Vineyard one summer, where there's a restaurant called the Chilmark Tavern, and the woman who runs that place made a chocolate pudding with whipped cream. I took some elements of what she does and riffed on several other versions, and voilà!

1½ cups heavy cream
½ cup whole milk
4 ounces semi-sweet chocolate chips
4 large egg yolks

3 tablespoons sugar
Pinch of kosher salt
Whipped cream, for serving
Cocoa powder, for serving

1. Preheat the oven to 300°F.

2. Place six 4-ounce ramekins in a large roasting pan and set aside.

3. In a heavy saucepan over medium heat, bring the heavy cream and milk to a boil. Remove from the heat.

4. Whisk in the chocolate chips until smooth.

5. In a large bowl, whisk together the egg yolks, sugar, and salt. Pour the hot chocolate mixture a little at a time into the yolk mixture, whisking to temper the eggs.

6. Strain the entire mixture through a fine-mesh sieve into a medium bowl, then ladle into the ramekins, dividing it equally.

7. Add hot tap water to the roasting pan, filling it halfway up the sides of the ramekins. Tightly cover the pan with foil, then poke a few holes in the foil to allow steam to escape.

continued

8. Bake until the edges are slightly set, 30 to 35 minutes. You'll know it's done when you tap the side of the pan with a towel and the centers jiggle.

9. Transfer the ramekins to a wire rack. Cool completely, about 30 minutes, then place in the refrigerator for at least 2 hours to chill.

10. Serve with a dollop of whipped cream and a dusting of cocoa powder.

PINEAPPLE UPSIDE-DOWN CAKE

SERVES 8 • **PREP TIME:** 15 minutes • **COOK TIME:** 50 minutes • **TOTAL TIME:** 1 hour 5 minutes

When I was about twelve years old, I borrowed one of Mom's old cookbooks to try a pineapple cake recipe. I realized that the brown sugar, butter, and pineapple had caramelized on the corners, and it was one of the best things I'd ever eaten in my life.

Already a chef in the making, I started experimenting with that recipe. (I think I was probably the only kid in my middle school who spent spare time trying to perfect cake recipes.) First I used pineapple rings, and then I switched to crushed pineapple. After some trial and error, I found that the crushed pineapple caramelized better than the circular rings. This recipe is all about the caramelization of the pineapple, brown sugar, and butter, and I haven't met a kid (or an adult) who doesn't love this cake.

8 tablespoons (1 stick) unsalted butter

1 cup packed dark brown sugar

One 20-ounce can crushed pineapple in juice, drained

9 maraschino cherries, stems removed

1⅓ cups all-purpose flour

1 cup granulated sugar

1½ teaspoons baking powder

½ teaspoon kosher salt

¾ cup whole milk

1 large egg

Whipped cream, for serving

1. Preheat the oven to 350°F.

2. In a small saucepan over low heat, melt the butter, then pour into a 9-inch square pan to coat.

3. Sprinkle the brown sugar evenly over the melted butter. Distribute the drained pineapple evenly over the brown sugar. Arrange the cherries on top of the pineapple.

continued

4. In a medium bowl, use a hand mixer on low speed to beat the flour, granulated sugar, baking powder, salt, milk, and egg, about 30 seconds. Increase the speed to high and beat for 3 minutes, scraping down the bowl occasionally, until the batter is smooth. Pour the batter over the pineapple and cherries.

5. Bake for 50 minutes, or until a toothpick comes out clean.

6. Immediately place a heatproof serving plate upside down over the cake. Invert the cake pan and leave the pan over the cake for a few minutes so the cake and brown sugar drop down. Remove the pan. Serve warm with whipped cream.

NANCY'S MURRAY MEMORY

A special memory of mine was coming home from school and being delighted that Mom had made fudge. This was a real special treat that the kids would enjoy and have eaten all up before Daddy got home from work. It was our secret, not to tell Daddy!

PLAGIARIZED APPLE CREAM CHEESE TORTE

SERVES 6 • **PREP TIME:** 20 minutes • **COOK TIME:** 45 minutes
TOTAL TIME: 3 hours 20 minutes (includes cooling time)

My sister Peggy's next-door neighbor had this incredible recipe for apple cheese torte, but when Peggy asked her for it, she refused for years to share it. Finally, that neighbor asked Peggy for something and Peggy responded, "I'll give it to you when you give me the recipe for the apple cheese torte." She agreed to this with the stipulation that Peggy was not allowed to serve it in their neighborhood, and she could not give anyone the recipe. Then this neighborhood cookbook came out called *The Bountiful Table*, which was a compilation of recipes from our home parish, St. Joseph's in Wilmette.

Under desserts, on page 200, there the recipe was . . . by another neighbor. My sister called and asked *her* where she got it and she said, "Okay, fine! I got it from the *Chicago Tribune*." We never could find it in the *Tribune*, and the dessert has transformed over the years. So here is our current version of what we now call Plagiarized Apple Cream Cheese Torte.

8 tablespoons (1 stick) unsalted butter

¾ cup sugar

¾ teaspoon vanilla extract

1 cup all-purpose flour

8 ounces cream cheese, softened

1 large egg

4 apples, such as Golden Delicious or Granny Smith, peeled, halved, cored, and cut into ¼-inch slices

½ teaspoon ground cinnamon

¾ cup slivered almonds

1. Preheat the oven to 450°F.

2. In a large bowl, use a hand mixer on medium speed to cream the butter, ¼ cup of the sugar, and ¼ teaspoon of the vanilla, about 3 minutes.

3. Slowly add in the flour, mixing on low speed, to form a smooth dough, 2 to 3 minutes. Spread the dough evenly on the bottom and 1½ inches up the sides of an 8- or 9-inch tart pan with a removable bottom.

4. In a separate medium bowl, mix the cream cheese and another ¼ cup of the sugar by hand until smooth, 1 to 2 minutes.

5. Add the egg and the remaining ½ teaspoon vanilla. Mix well for 2 minutes and spread over the bottom of the pastry-lined pan.

6. In a separate bowl, mix together the apples, the remaining ¼ cup sugar, and the cinnamon. Spoon the apples over the cream cheese layer.

7. Sprinkle the top with the almonds. Bake for 10 minutes, then reduce the heat to 400°F and bake for 25 minutes, or until lightly golden brown.

8. Loosen the torte from the rim and let it rest on a wire rack for about 15 minutes. Refrigerate for 2 hours before serving.

LAURA'S MURRAY MEMORY

Thinking of Mom at the kitchen sink always brings a smile—our sink was located under a window that overlooked the backyard, and it was one of Mom's favorite spots. If someone else was in the room, she might comment on the need to mow the lawn or to do some cleanup, or she'd find the joy of seeing a cardinal hanging on the swinging branch of the willow. Most of all, it was a thing of beauty to watch how she could enjoy a carton of ice cream at the sink. Thinking we were unaware, she'd work the spoon along the square to get the softest and easiest part with very little movement. She did this in plain sight, and it was genius. You've got a house full of a million kids, and you want a treat for yourself—where do you go to hide? *The kitchen sink*—where dishes needed to be washed. Her mantra was, "Nothing can cure whatever ails you better than soapy, hot dishwater," but finding any kids hanging around the kitchen sink just wasn't a thing. So while we were laughing and teasing her, she was laughing at us.

10

THE 19TH HOLE: COCKTAILS

BLAME IT ON THE CALVADOS

When my parents occasionally had a drink, it was a highball or an old-fashioned (and you'll see that recipe on page 178). But when I was growing up, we didn't have big parties where liquor was involved. However, when the kids all got older, we discovered we all enjoy—and make—a good cocktail. It's become a nice way to celebrate birthdays, reunions, all that.

In fact, one of our favorite things to do when we get together after not seeing each other for a while is go out to a restaurant. But restaurant drinks can be *strong*, and there was one time when a dessert beverage caused a divide *so* huge it has now become an urban legend that is actually true. Here's what happened . . .

When Brian's wife, Tina, lost her father, a group of us planned to go to the memorial service in Kansas City. I had been living in Chicago, staying with Laura and her husband, Bob, who had bought the house where we all grew up. Billy came in a few days early and stayed with me while Bob and Laura drove down to Kansas City to spend time with Brian and Tina before the service.

Billy and I decided that a round of golf was in order before we had to pick up Nancy at the train station. She's a Dominican nun and was coming to the funeral with us in Kansas City. While Billy was putting on his shoes, he looked around the living room.

"You know, we should move around all the furniture," he said.

"No. That's a very bad idea," I said.

My brother-in-law Bob is one of my favorite people in the world. But he likes his things to be in their proper place. Moving all the furniture would not go over well.

Bill and I went to Indian Hill Country Club and played 18 holes before picking up Nancy. We drove to the Wilmette train station—and there's

Nancy, who has traveled with this suitcase that's the size of a small car and filled with these nun shoes that weigh about eight pounds apiece. Billy and I both had to lift that thing to get it into the trunk, and I was thinking, *What does she do when her brothers aren't here?* It was quite a sight.

We went out to dinner, where the food and wine were flowing. After dinner, they brought out glasses of Calvados. If you've never had it, Calvados is a kind of brandy made from apples that hails from Normandy, France. Like Champagne, it has to be grown in a certain region in order for it to have the Calvados name. It's very good and sweet, the kind of drink you save for a special occasion.

While we were enjoying the brandy, Billy started telling Nancy about his idea of moving the furniture.

"Bob needs a good laugh," he said.

"No, that's a bad idea," I said.

But then the Calvados kicked in.

We got home and were listening to Bruce Hornsby's "Fortunate Son / Comfortably Numb" when Billy got up and started moving furniture. At first, I thought he would switch just a couple of chairs, but when he tried to lift the couch, I knew that if I didn't help, he would be breaking furniture—which would be much worse. The next thing I knew, I was an accomplice. The dining room wound up in the family room, the kitchen in the living room, and the living room in the dining room. Basically, the whole first floor got rearranged. We finally got tired and went to bed, but neither of us got much sleep.

The next morning, we got up and met in the hallway upstairs, just outside the bedroom doors. This was the place where I spent my youth—I felt like I was twelve years old again, and I was about to be grounded. We shared a guilty moment of eye contact before going downstairs to assess the damage.

The first thing I saw when I came down the stairs was the butcher's block table from the kitchen in the center of the living room. I knew we'd just done a really bad thing. But Billy and I couldn't stop giggling. And then reality set in: *How would we move this furniture back in place before Bob and Laura came home in a couple of days?* We had to hit the road that morning in order to make it to the service, and we just didn't have time to undo our dirty work.

"I'll call Bubba," Billy said. Bubba was an old friend, but we weren't sure he'd be able to put the furniture back where it belonged before Bob and Laura got home.

Billy, Nancy, and I left for Kansas City to pay our respects and went the whole weekend without saying a word.

Sunday morning rolled around, and I didn't see Bob and Laura. We found out they'd already started driving back to Chicago. I looked at Billy and said, "We are in so much trouble." There was no way for us to beat them home since they'd already left, and Bubba wasn't able to get into the house either. We were toast.

When Bob saw the work of his brothers-in-law, he went right into the family room (which was now the dining room), took a seat, and didn't say a word for *two hours*. We called a florist near their house and ordered the biggest arrangement they had. It didn't matter. Bob answered the door for the flower delivery, and said, "These must be for you, Laura, because they can't possibly be for me."

It took weeks to get Laura to talk to me. In their minds, I was Benedict Arnold, and justifiably so. I wrote Bob a heartfelt letter and apologized, and eventually we smoothed things over.

The following Christmas, Bob and Laura got me and Billy a set of T-shirts that said: MURRAY BROTHERS MOVING. WE WON'T MOVE IT 'TIL YOU LEAVE. That's when I knew we were going to be okay.

But I won't be drinking any Calvados for a while.

The following recipes are some of my favorites, and brandy-free, for good reason! From Lucille's Old-Fashioned (page 178) to the proven Bloody Bull (page 184) hangover cure, all these drinks are simple but impressive.

But do yourself a favor: Don't drink too much and rearrange the furniture. It never turns out well.

BRIAN'S MURRAY MEMORY

As I recall, Andy was working at Mortimer's restaurant. John Belushi, my brother Johnny, and I stopped in for a late bite. Andy came out from the kitchen to say hi and tell us, "No free drinks for you guys, but I'll comp all your desserts." After an excellent meal, while I was nursing a pricey cognac and Johnny sipped a Grand Marnier, we watched Belushi polish off a crème brûlée, chocolate mousse, order of profiteroles, the ice cream of the day, and a crêpe Suzette. I knew Andy had misread his customers, because while Johnny and I were known to put away a few drinks, Belushi was just a two-beer guy. And once, I had personally witnessed him, after polishing off a three-layer chocolate cake that his wife, Judy, had hidden in the cupboard, look up, as if coming out of a trance, and utter the immortal words of the famous Alka-Seltzer commercial: "I can't believe I ate the whole thing."

19TH HOLE

The 19th Hole cocktail is a signature delight at Murray Bros. Caddyshack. This peach and lemony drink is perfect . . . well, everywhere. It's refreshing enough to brighten up anyone's day—or perk up their golf game. It certainly has for me! I especially love serving this at a barbecue or pool party.

2 ounces peach vodka

½ ounce Aperol

1 ounce simple syrup

1 ounce fresh lemon juice

Ice, for straining

Lemon twist, to garnish

1. Build the cocktail in a Boston shaker. Shake for 10 seconds.
2. Strain over ice in a tall glass. Garnish with a lemon twist.

LUCILLE'S OLD-FASHIONED

The original old-fashioned was created at the Pendennis Club in Louisville, Kentucky. There are two types of old-fashioned drinkers: those who muddle the fruit and those who don't. I'm on the muddling side of things—it adds so much flavor! When our family went out for dinner, Lucille would order an old-fashioned, so I created this drink at my restaurant in her honor.

1 teaspoon sugar

A few dashes of bitters

2 orange slices

2 maraschino cherries

1 tablespoon soda water

2½ ounces rye or bourbon whiskey

1 teaspoon water (optional)

1. In the bottom of an old-fashioned glass, use a muddler to muddle the sugar, bitters, 1 of the orange slices, 1 of the maraschino cherries, and the soda water.
2. Remove and discard the muddled orange and cherry. Add the rye and, if you like, water, but be careful not to drown the drink. Too much water will make it a light caramel color.
3. Garnish with the remaining orange slice and cherry.

JOEL'S MURRAY MEMORY

We went to *Saturday Night Live* in New York to see Billy one time when Milton Berle was the host. We wound up at the Tap A Keg next to the Ed Sullivan Theater. Mom was watching people do these inverse margaritas at the bar, so she got up there, and they poured all the ingredients in her mouth, and 15 minutes later, she decided to do another one. She proceeded to dance to "Some Girls" by the Rolling Stones, and she was really cutting a rug. I will never forget that.

PAINKILLER

The first time I had a painkiller was with my nephew Jackson at the Rutledge Cab Company in Charleston, South Carolina. We were celebrating his twenty-first birthday, and when I saw the name of the drink on the menu, I thought, *What's that?* One sip in, and we were feeling no pain whatsoever. I knew I wanted to bring this drink to my restaurant. Here's our version of this tropical cocktail.

2 ounces white rum

2 ounces Coco López cream of coconut

1 ounce pineapple juice

1 ounce orange juice

Ice, for straining

Dash of ground nutmeg, for garnish

1. Build the cocktail in a Boston shaker. Shake for 10 seconds.
2. Strain over ice in a large rocks glass.
3. Garnish with the nutmeg.

TRANSFUSION

This drink is unusual—and so refreshing! I tried it for the first time on a golf course in New Jersey and immediately knew we had to create our own version for the restaurant. It has become so popular that we now offer it in cans for sale in several stores across the country. I think it's the lime juice that makes it so light, but the grape juice adds a nice touch too. This cocktail is built in either an old-fashioned glass or a Moscow mule copper mug.

2 ounces vodka

1 ounce grape juice (Concord grape juice is the best)

Ice, for serving

Juice of ½ lime

4 ounces ginger beer

1 lime slice or a pinch of grated peeled fresh ginger, for garnish (see Chef Andy's Note)

1. Pour the vodka and grape juice into an old-fashioned glass or a Moscow mule copper mug filled with ice.
2. Pour the lime juice over the cocktail, add the ginger beer, and stir.
3. Garnish with a slice of lime or fresh ginger.

CHEF ANDY'S NOTE: *Fresh ginger is a nice addition if I have any on hand in the kitchen. You can grate it on top of the cocktail, or even muddle some inside the drink.*

BLOODY BULL

For our Sunday brunches at Mortimer's, we used to do something really unique with our Bloody Marys—add beef broth. I know it may seem strange, but the way I see it, people are putting entire pizzas on top of their Bloodys these days. Nothing is off limits.

One Sunday, we had a regular who came in at 11:30 A.M., and had 22 Bloody Bulls. *Twenty-two!* The staff started taking bets to see how many more he could handle. He surprised us all and stayed until 9:00 P.M. He was definitely a professional. After his twenty-second, he wobbled outside and hailed a cab, and that was that.

But the beef broth really helps if you're hung over—something about the sodium and protein. I love this combination. And be sure you don't skimp on the ice—this one needs ice, and lots of it.

3 ounces beef broth

3 ounces Bloody Mary mix

2 ounces vodka

1 tablespoon Worcestershire sauce

Plenty of ice

1 lime wedge, for garnish

1. Mix the ingredients together in a shaker and shake well. Pour into a tall glass over ice.

2. Add a wedge of lime and any preferred garnishes. Serve.

BONUS MENUS

Now, I love all these dishes on their own—but I'm a chef, so of course I designed some menus. These are great to pile together (more on "piling on" in a bit . . .).

CADDYSHACK FAN

Caddyshack Golf Balls 45

Grilled Pimento Cheese Sandwich 84

19th Hole 174

Key Lime Pie 156

WE LOVE LUCILLE

Lucille's Salad 53

Lucille's Fried Chicken 110

Lucille's Old-Fashioned 178

Plagiarized Apple Cream Cheese Torte 166

BRUNCH OF CHAMPIONS

Corn Fritters with Salmon Roe 56

Murray French Toast 26

Transfusion 182

HANGOVER CURE

At least 2 Bloody Bulls 184

Chicken Hash 28

THE BIG GAME

Peggy's Baked Beans 49

Lasagna with Italian Sausage 141

Pulled Pork Sandwich or Turkey-Artichoke Sandwich 91 or 94

Pineapple Upside-Down Cake 163

Painkiller 180

THE KIDS' TABLE

Hot Nuts 58

Bill Blass Meat Loaf 107

Homage to Elvis Cookie 158

FOR THE LOVERS

French Onion Soup 73

Frank Sinatra's Dover Sole 122

Chocolate Pots de Crème 161

Your favorite bottle of white wine or champagne

THE BOSS IS COMING TO DINNER

Red Radish Spread 51

Potatoes Dauphinoise 60

Rack of Lamb 104

Chocolate Pots de Crème 161

JOHNNY'S MURRAY MEMORY

Our family had this weird tradition where we would pile on someone, to the point of submission. I'm not kidding—we would literally pin someone down on the bed, and everyone would climb on top until the smothered person managed to scream enough to be released. It was intended to be an act of endearment, but apparently not everybody thought it was funny or endearing. One night, we were at a party after *Saturday Night Live* in New York, and Billy Joel was there with us, and my brother Bill just got this look in his eye. The next thing I knew, Andy, Bill, and I all piled onto Billy Joel, right there on the host's bed. I mean, we just tackled the guy. He managed to escape, but he could not get out of that party fast enough! I've never seen Billy Joel again.

Johnny, Brian, and the back of Joel's head "piling on" Mom.
(We would go easy on Lucille.)

ACKNOWLEDGMENTS

This book would not have been possible without a lot of help from many.

First, I need to thank Karen Duffy. Three years ago, I was cooking Thanksgiving dinner at my brother Billy's house, and an attractive woman proceeded to pull up a chair in the kitchen. She spent the next couple of hours chatting with me while I cooked. After dinner, she came up to me and said, "You should really write a cookbook." I immediately thought I needed to start drinking whatever she'd been having. I begged off, saying my plate was quite full and maybe it was something we could discuss after the new year. Well, after three different psychics in a ten-day period told me I was going to write a book (that's a whole other conversation), I called her for advice, and she introduced me to her, and now my, agent.

David Vigliano, agent extraordinaire, took my call and said, "Yes, Duff has been telling me about you." He had a wonderful sense of humor, and I figured that if I just kept him laughing, something good would follow. In a matter of a couple of months, I had put together a sample idea for the book and we were off to the races. I'm just so happy he was an easy laugh.

To my team at HarperCollins / Dey Street Books led by Carrie Thornton, the person who made the decision to go with my idea. For her, I am so grateful. I was lucky enough that she assigned Anna Montague as my wonderful book editor. She is kind, smart, and has been very patient dealing with my procrastination.

To Paul Strabbing and Johanna Lowe for their food photography and styling, making all the dishes look so delicious.

To my sisters, Nancy, Peggy, and Laura, whom I adore and without whose help everything about this project would be lacking. To my brothers, Ed, Brian, Billy, Johnny, and Joel, who have all contributed to this book and, more importantly, my life.

There are a lot of people I've worked with and learned from along the way, starting with the Parker's gentlemen, Fred White and George Shelton, who made me realize I so enjoyed cooking. Eric and Kitty Pergeaux gave me my first serious job on Shelter Island, and Marcel Iatoni kept that love of French cooking alive in me. And when I arrived at Mortimer's, Timmy Wagner took me under his wing and became a good friend. Then came Stephen Attoe, who at first seemed like a stern taskmaster, but he became the person who taught me self-discipline—which was sorely lacking. I was lucky enough to work with Alison Abels, Neal Myers, Johnny Marsh, David Bailie, and, of course, Glenn Bernbaum. Many thanks to my friends Don Pintabona, Marty Shapiro, and Drew Nieporent of Tribeca Grill. And I can't forget my Murray Bros. Caddyshack family: my business partner and friend, Mac Haskell, who allows me to ride his coattails; and Renee Shuey, Susan Gibson, Mike Avella, and Ryan Prendergastand, who all make the Murray Bros. Caddyshack restaurants run like fine watches. To my brother-from-another-mother, Chris Seely, for getting things done. Thanks to Kathy Worthington for cleaning up the grammatical mistakes. And last, but definitely not least, to Jenniffer Weigel, without whose constant help and encouragement, none of this would have been possible.

Thank you all!

INDEX

FIRST EDITION

DESIGNED BY RENATA DE OLIVEIRA

Food photography by Paul Strabbing
Food styling by Johanna Lowe
Golf course photographs courtesy of William Murray Golf
All other family photographs courtesy of the Murray family
Geometric pattern by Lily Sab/Shuttersotck

Library of Congress Cataloging-in-Publication Data has been applied for.

ISBN 978-0-06-314100-1

22 23 24 25 26   WOR   10 9 8 7 6 5 4 3 2 1